THE PEDESTRIAN REVOLUTION

THE PEDESTRIAN REVOLUTION

STREETS WITHOUT CARS

SIMON BREINES
WILLIAM J. DEAN

Vintage Books
A Division of Random House, New York

From the standpoint of the pedestrian, God made the open country, man made the city, and there is simply no walking in the suburbs. SIMEON STRUNSKY in *No Mean City*

VINTAGE BOOKS EDITION 1974

First Edition

Copyright © 1974 by Simon Breines and William J. Dean

All rights reserved under International and Pan-American Copyright Conventions. Published in the United States by Random House, Inc., New York, and simultaneously in Canada by Random House of Canada Limited, Toronto.

Library of Congress Cataloging in Publication Data

Breines, Simon. The pedestrian revolution.

Includes bibliographical references. 1. Pedestrian facilities design. 2. Pedestrians.

I. Dean, William J., 1937– joint author. II. Title.

TE279.5.B7   625.8'8   74–9177   ISBN 0-394-71305-2

Manufactured in the United States of America

ACKNOWLEDGMENTS

New York Chapter, American Institute of Architects, which awarded its 1947 Arnold W. Brunner Scholarship to Simon Breines for a book on planning for pedestrians.

The late John P. Dean, professor of sociology, Cornell University, who collaborated with Simon Breines on a draft manuscript, "City People on the Move," in 1949. There was little interest among publishers in the subject at that time.

Elisabeth Coit, friend, colleague and member of the Brunner Scholarship Committee in 1965, who kept the idea of the book alive all these years with her encouragement, research and criticism.

Ralph Pomerance, partner in the architectural firm of Pomerance & Breines, who shares a continuing interest in pedestrianism and contributed many ideas and clarifications to the present book.

Citizens Union, a civic organization in New York City, which brought William J. Dean and Simon Breines together in 1966. They discovered a common interest in cities and walking, so that the burgeoning pedestrian revolution made their collaboration on this book natural and timely.

The authors are grateful to Jason Epstein, Vice-President of Random House, without whose encouragement and support there would be no book; to Susan Bolotin, Education Director at Vintage Books, for her perceptive suggestions and skillful editorial guidance; to Jack Ribik, James Cosby and Robert Scudellari, who all were involved with the art direction of the book; and to Jacqueline Adato, artist, and Robert Cordes, mapmaker.

To Frederick and Paula Morgan, whose enthusiasm over the exciting possibilities for freeing urban design from the tyranny of the gridiron street pattern led them to advocate the need for a book on the subject.

To Sally Forbes, picture researcher, who gathered, with expertness and imagination, many of the pictures used in this book.

To Bonita Sandrowitz, who typed and typed and typed.

And to the Scarsdale Public Library, whose staff, particularly Mrs. Hope Dershowitz, was most helpful with books and references.

CONTENTS

THE PEDESTRIAN REVOLUTION

CHAPTER 1

THE PEDESTRIAN REVOLUTION

A new day is dawning for the pedestrian. Footpower has begun to challenge horsepower. World-wide action against unrestrained automobile use in congested urban centers heralds the arrival of the Pedestrian Revolution. Geography is no barrier to the movement, nor is ideology. Vehicle-free pedestrian areas exist in Western cities as diverse as New York, London, Paris, Munich, Copenhagen, Rome and Vienna. A section of Warsaw's old town is set aside for pedestrian use, and the Leningrad City Soviet has authorized the closing of Nevsky Prospect, the city's main avenue, to vehicular traffic.

Streets without cars are popular in Mexico City. *Pedonalizzazione*—the restitution of streets to the pedestrian—is a movement in Italy.[1] In Stockholm, the

Arc de Triomphe, Paris. The march of the victorious automobiles in celebration of their capture of the streets of Paris. What a "triumph"!

areas reserved for pedestrian use are called "walking streets"; in Tokyo, "pedestrian paradises."

Urban society's growing disenchantment with the automobile, and the congestion it causes, is a major factor behind the Pedestrian Revolution. Henry Ford described his first gasoline buggy as "something of a nuisance, for it made a racket and scared horses." Even in his wildest dreams he could not have foreseen the nuisance it has become—to people!

The automobile has penetrated virtually every crack and crevice of our cities.

"Think'st thou the time will ever come when all the earth shall be paved?" asks a character in Herman Melville's novel *Pierre*. Pierre responds, "Thank God, that can never be!" Today Pierre's response might be given with less assurance. A cartoon in the French newspaper *Le Monde* showing an expressway plunging through the doors of Notre Dame Cathedral, with a road sign forbidding horn-tooting during

Oxford Street, London—a tribute to the survival power of the urban pedestrian. Despite the lack of walking space, the hazards of traffic and the noise and air pollution, the shopper still manages to supply the purchasing power that keeps this street the famous shopping mart that it is. But can this process continue under such adverse circumstances? The answer is no. Oxford Street is now closed to private vehicles.

The Roman Colosseum, built nearly two thousand years ago, has resisted barbarian raids, earthquakes and other ravages of time, but now is crumbling under the relentless onslaught of traffic. The scaffolding is necessary because Colosseum stones have been loosened by the constant vibration of vehicles.

mass, comes closer to the truth. We are slaves to wheels, just as in Greek mythology Ixion, for his impious attempt to seduce Hera, was chained to a wheel by Zeus and condemned to revolve in Hades.

Designed to travel at speeds in excess of one mile a minute, the automobile op-

erates best on a reasonably clear, uninterrupted road. Street intersections, traffic signals, the crush of vehicles and of crowds, all serve to reduce dramatically the automobile's speed and efficiency. In urban centers, where average speeds plunge to five miles per hour or less, it is a fish out of water. Horse-drawn vehicles at the turn of the century moved through city streets at a faster rate.[2]

The driver of a crippled motor vehicle is all too aware of these conditions, as is the pedestrian anxiously threading his way through traffic. Even high government officials are learning about them. Caught in a massive London traffic jam, Edward Heath, at that time Prime Minister of Britain, could only reach his official residence at No. 10 Downing Street by abandoning his limousine and walking. When he complained to the head of the Greater London Council, the unflappable local government official told the Prime Minister, "It has happened before and it will happen again."

And so it will, though the car may become smaller, cleaner and quieter. Henry Ford II, hardly a disinterested observer, writes:

None of these changes will do much to relieve traffic congestion or make it easier to get around in cities. . . . For all its flexibility, the car is not the best possible way to get to or move around in very busy places.[3]

THE PEDESTRIAN REVOLUTION

"Make way for a pedestrian!"

DRAWING BY GEO. PRICE; © 1967 THE NEW YORKER MAGAZINE, INC.

Guerrilla warfare in the Pedestrian Revolution.

The convergence of cars, trucks and buses in urban centers results in sheer vehicular hell. In the midst of this chaos, one easily forgets that cities exist for the care and culture of people, not the passage of motor vehicles.

The economic cost of congestion—in time lost, manpower and fuel—runs into the billions. The social cost includes living under continual stress from intimidation by large, fast, noisy vehicles out of scale with their surroundings; often the cost is death itself.*

---

* In New York City, the casualty figures seem more appropriate for a battlefield communiqué than a Traffic Department report. 1973 casualties: 412 pedestrian deaths and 14,424 pedestrian injuries.

Oxford Street, London's major shopping thoroughfare, which enjoyed the dubious reputation of the most dangerous street in Europe, numbered three hundred pedestrian casualties a year until—as much for humanitarian as for traffic reasons—private cars were banned.[4] Today, on Oxford Street at least, a pedestrian is no longer defined as one who, while afoot, is struck, injured or put to death by an automobile or other gasoline-driven vehicle.[5]

The provision of safe and inviting walking facilities would reduce much of today's urban congestion, since walking is the most efficient way to move large numbers of people for short distances. A pedestrian uses twenty times less space than an automobile. Lewis Mumford, a pioneer in the study of cities, estimates that the entire daytime population of historic Boston could assemble by foot on Boston Common in less than an hour if the streets were clear of traffic. Transportation by automobile would take many hours, and some Bostonians would never arrive at all, unless they abandoned their unparkable vehicles.

Energy and environmental concerns are other root causes of the Pedestrian Revolution. The amount of energy our nation expends on the transportation of people and goods is prodigious. Cars and trucks in the United States burn 40 percent of all the petroleum used in America. For the

sole purpose of transportation, 211 million Americans use more energy than 1.3 billion Indians and Chinese use for all purposes combined.

Footpower is a vast, neglected energy source. It is the most important of all forms of urban transport, contends Colin Buchanan, author of the report *Traffic in Towns,* the landmark study of traffic in Britain and its effect on urban living:

Walking accounts for a vast amount of movement—all the final distribution from bus stops, parking places, and stations, and a multitude of casual comings and goings some of which (window shopping, for example) are almost the essence of urban life. Nor is walking to be neglected as a medium for carrying goods —small in individual loads, but vast in aggregate.

Unlike the glamour fuels of the future— the winds, the tides, the sun and the heat of the earth—the widespread use of which may be decades away, if ever realizable at all, footpower is available in abundance here and now.

Car remover at work in London. "Far from living in 'the second machine age,' " writes British journalist and broadcaster Malcolm MacEwen, "we are in fact entering the first period of human revolt *against* unrestrained and misdirected science and technology."

Fifth Avenue, New York City. This pedestrian takeover of the world-famous avenue, even if only for a day, is a premonition of things to come.

At present, when almost nothing is done to encourage walking, hundreds of thousands of additional vehicles would be needed to do the work of pedestrians. During the midday hours in Manhattan's central business district, for example, more than two thirds of all surface travel occurs on foot, although only one third of the circulation space is available to pedestrians.[6] Where pedestrian travel is encouraged, the results are startling. Following the closing of sections of Munich's center to motor vehicles, pedestrian traffic increased by 60 percent.[7] Significant reductions in conventional fuel use would accompany increases in pedestrian activity.

Few cities are not plagued by vehicular pollutants. In New York City the transportation of people and goods accounts for roughly 95 percent of the carbon-monoxide emissions, 65 percent of the hydrocarbons, 40 percent of the nitrogen oxides, and 15 percent of the particulates in the city's air, as well as significant doses of toxic heavy metals.[8] The foul air New Yorkers breathe is a serious health hazard. A policy of pedestrian engineering can make an important difference to a city's air quality. Past experimental closings of sections of New York's Fifth and Madison avenues to motor vehicles have resulted in major reductions of carbon monoxide and other pollutants.

Traffic in urban centers produces noise levels comparable to the noise in a factory, with peaks classified as deafening, the man-made equivalent of thunder. Closing a street to motor vehicles reduces noise to the level of ordinary conversation.

Visual pollution is another environmental factor. Whether moving or stationary, the automobile dominates every street scene. Buildings have the appearance of rising not from the streets, but from the roofs of cars. Not even areas of architectural or historical interest are spared. The paraphernalia associated with automobiles—traffic lights, street signs, parking meters—contribute to the visual assault.

To replace an acoustically harsh soundscape with the sounds of man, such as the human voice; the smell of petroleum products with, if not a hint of sweet fields and the sea in the breeze, at least purer air; the relentless, rushing motion of cars with vehicle-free islands, where safety and calm can be enjoyed; to fully utilize an available, nonpolluting energy source, are the environmental goals of the Pedestrian Revolution.

Pedestrianism enhances our physical well-being both by reducing air and noise pollution and by encouraging, through the creation of urban strollways and urban bikeways, the greater use of footpower. George Macaulay Trevelyan enjoyed the best medical advice in the world. "I have two doctors," the British historian wrote, "my left leg and my right leg." It is no mere coincidence that between 1930 and 1960, when walking became a lost skill as Americans started to drive in large numbers, that deaths resulting from coronary disease increased 2,000 percent.[9]

For too long we have treated the auto-

Strøget, Copenhagen. The most civilized street in the most civilized of cities.

mobile as a sacred cow, allowing it to roam anywhere while we watched it take over our cities. Nothing spent in its service has been begrudged. But now the Pedestrian Revolution is upon us! Two Paris incidents dramatize the change.

The first, in 1967: The policeman waving on the eternal traffic at the Place Charles de Gaulle, from which twelve avenues radiate from the Arc de Triomphe, gruffly responds to a query concerning pe-

Tokyo. An Asian manifestation of the Pedestrian Revolution. The sign on the traffic barrier reads: "Cars—Do Not Enter."

destrian privileges, "Pedestrians, they went out in 1900."

The second, in 1974: A police prefect directs his men to forbid cars entry to the Latin Quarter, on the Left Bank of the Seine. "Make way for the pedestrians!" police tell motorists.

But the car cannot be disinvented. And banning the car entirely is no answer. Few people today have not had their lives enriched by the automobile. Public transportation, at least in its present form, cannot match the automobile for comfort or flexibility.

The solution is to exploit the advantages of foot and wheel in areas where each operates better. On the basis of such a policy, the unrestrained use of the automobile in cities would end. By excluding the car from areas of the highest density, where it cannot compete with pedestrians for short-distance trips or with mass transportation for longer trips, and freeing it for use in areas of lower density and for intercity travel, pedestrian engineering places the automobile in a setting where it can function efficiently.

When we lavish the attention on the pedestrian we now accord only to the automobile, we will find, as Joseph Wood

Krutch has noted, that legs are an even more remarkable invention than the wheel. Pedestrians are, as Mumford puts it, the greatest self-propelling vehicle of all.

The renaissance of the street will not, of course, cure all urban ills. The grinding problems of poverty and crime will remain. But streets are important. They comprise one third of the total area in cities, and provide every city with its main public places and major movement system. Urban dwellers, every day of their lives, experience, use, view and feel them. "Think of a city and what comes to mind?" asks Jane Jacobs, the noted urban critic, in *The Death and Life of Great American Cities*. To her own question she responds: "Its streets. If a city's streets look interesting, the city looks interesting; if they look dull, the city looks dull." Improve streets and you affect beneficially the daily life of every urban resident.

Pedestrianism has nothing to do with nostalgia for the past or a Puritan emphasis on exercise. The goal of the walking city is to increase the opportunities for every resident to enjoy the richness of urban life. People should have the right to walk to work, to school, to stores, under safe, pleasant and healthy conditions; to converse with friends without the noise or threat of cars; to escape the summer heat along tree-shaded avenues; to relax on benches and survey the passing stream of life.

The Pedestrian Revolution has arrived! Yet to date, the response to it has brought forth little more than an occasional pedestrian refuge scattered hither and yon. The Pedestrian Revolution needs direction and a plan.

In the chapters which follow, we try to fill this void. In our effort to do so, we are fortunate to be able to draw upon the pioneering work of perceptive urban thinkers like Lewis Mumford, Colin Buchanan and Jane Jacobs, who years ago recognized the close relationship of decent walking conditions to civilized urban life.

CHAPTER II
THE PEDESTRIAN IN HISTORY

Many of the modern words we associate with walking have deep roots in history.

In classical Athens, walking was part of the discipline of two philosophical schools —the Peripatetic and the Stoic.[1] The origin of "peripatetic" is the Greek word *peripatos,* meaning "to walk about." Aristotle, who founded the Peripatetic School, instructed his students as he and they strolled through the shaded grove of the Lyceum. His disciples were called Peripatetics, and the word has come down to us as meaning "given to walking about."

The Stoics took their name from *stoa,*

For the modern visitor to Athens, the Acropolis serves as the center of attention. But in ancient Athens, the busiest place in the city was the *agora,* the "gathering place," an open public space located below the Acropolis. Here was "downtown" Athens, a pedestrian area, with its markets, shrines and government building. Finley Hooper writes in *Greek Realities:* "The commingling of the Athenians in the *agora* was one of the pleasant graces of life they took for granted."

meaning "roofed colonnade." The stoas were built to screen shops and pedestrians from the sun. It was in the shade of a stoa that Zeno of Citium and the other Stoic philosophers of the third century B.C. held forth.[2]

In his *Dictionary*, Dr. Johnson gives the origin of the word "saunter": "From the idle people who roved about the country, and asked charity under pretense of going *à la sainte terre*, to the holy land." People would point them out, saying, "There goes a Sainte-Terrer," a saunterer, a Holy-Lander. Thus, there is a historical basis for Henry David Thoreau writing: "Every walk is a sort of crusade preached by some Peter the Hermit in us, to go forth and reconquer this Holy Land from the hands of the Infidels."

The term "mall" has close associations with London. A mall is a wooden mallet, and the old game of pall-mall is similar to modern croquet. Mall also is the word for the alleys where the game was played. Pall Mall, the center of club activity in London, is on the site of a former pall-mall alley. The word came to refer to a shaded walk, such as the Mall in London's St. James's Park, and more recently, a pedestrian area, with or without an abundance of shade-producing trees.

Many Spanish cities have a public space for walking called a *rambla*. The word comes from the Arabic word *ramla*, meaning "dry riverbed." (In parts of Spain, except during the spring, the riverbeds are dry, making for pleasant walking on the sand.) In the evening, it is customary for the populace to stroll along the *rambla*, or avenue, chatting with friends. The *rambla* provides parents with the opportunity to place their eligible daughters on view. (The English word "ramble" has a similar origin.) World-famous are the

Ramblas in Barcelona, and a heavily wooded area called the Ramble in New York's Central Park.

From the time of the earliest cities until the nineteenth century, urban planners took care to scale the city to man and to his natural ability for movement on his own two feet. London today is about 650 times as large as the area covered by medieval London. Rome, when surrounded by the Aurelian Wall in A.D. 274, comprised little more than five square miles.[3]

Despite the small area to traverse, pedestrians in Rome had their problems. The congestion in Rome's streets led Julius Caesar, as one of his first acts on seizing power in 49 B.C., to ban carts and chariots from the city between sunrise and sunset. His subjects bitterly complained that the intensive vehicle activity at night made sleep impossible. More than a century and a half later, the Latin poet Juvenal describes the abuse he suffers as a Roman pedestrian:

We are blocked by a surging crowd in front, and by a dense mass of people pressing in on us from behind: one man digs an elbow into me, another a sedan-pole; one bangs a beam, another a wine-cask, against my head. My legs are beplastered with mud; huge feet trample on me from every side, and a soldier plants his hobnails firmly on my toe.[4]

Sixteen miles of colonnaded streets wound through fourth-century Antioch. The social function and value of such thoroughfares were well recognized, as this excerpt on Antioch from the oration

Pompeii. The stepping stones across this ancient city street raise the walker above the dust and mud; mute witness to Pompeii's concern for pedestrians, as was the city's Forum, a pedestrian mall, closed to wheeled traffic by the use of bollards.

of Libanius indicates:

Well, it seems to me that the pleasantest, yes, and most profitable side of city life is society and human intercourse, and that, by Zeus, is truly a city where these are most found. It is good to talk and better to listen, and best of all to give advice, to sympathize with one's friends' experiences, sharing their joys and sorrows and getting like sympathy from them —these and countless other blessings come of a man's meeting his fellows. People in other cities who have no colonnades before their houses are kept apart by bad weather; nominally, they live in the same town, but in fact they are as remote from each other as if they lived in different towns. ... Whereas people in cities lose the habit of intimacy the further they live apart, with us, on the other hand, the habit of friendship is matured by constant intercourse and develops here as much as it diminishes there.[5]

The medieval street, narrow and winding, served primarily as a pedestrian way. Since the needs of wheeled traffic were secondary, it made sense to let streets follow nature's contours rather than to grade them. The streets also served a military purpose. During these disordered times, the complexity of the street system was

Milan in the Middle Ages. With footpower as the principal means of movement, walking distance served as an effective limit on urban expansion. Medieval street patterns tended to be circular and radial. The straight avenues of the gridiron system came later as a response to the demands of fast-traveling, horse-drawn carriages.

MEDIOLANVM

Venice, with its ninety miles of walkways, provides a splendid urban environment for pedestrians. Today, as in past centuries, the Piazza San Marco serves as an open public place for informal gathering and ceremony. Bernard Rudofsky in *Streets for People* points out that many years ago pedestrian ascendancy over the square was briefly challenged. The Venetian gentry, enamored of horses, would gallop about the Piazza San Marco. They became such a nuisance to walkers that restrictions were imposed; riders had to dismount and tie their horses to bushes where the Clock Tower now stands.

prized as a means of defense in case the enemy penetrated the outer wall.[6]

The medieval planner did not ignore aesthetic considerations. Fritz Rörig writes in *The Medieval Town:*

It is not by pure chance that we get again and again in the Middle Ages such wonderful street endings—here a church façade or there a group of market and town buildings; all this would not have been possible if the streets had not been planned from the beginning in such a way that our gaze falls continually on the buildings stretched out in front of us, and never gets lost in the bleak emptiness of a dead-straight, open-ended street.[7]

In terms of urban amenities, tenth-century Moorish Spain far surpassed Christian Europe. In Cordova, at night, one could travel for ten miles by the light of street lamps. The city was famous for its gardens and promenades. Its streets were paved.[8] (Streets in Paris did not lose their natural underfooting until 1184, when King Philip Augustus paved the roadway in front of the Louvre.)

In the hands of the medieval paver, paving became an art. The pride and pleasure in streets and public spaces found expression in their decoration. Paving designs could be functional, delineating the use of the space, or purely aesthetic, as with the famous paved sunburst of Siena's Piazza del Campo.

But medieval streets were far from ideal. While the narrow, curving streets may have broken the force of winter winds, and been a refuge from the summer's heat, they were dirty and dark, producing an acute sense of claustrophobia. The passing pedestrian might have the contents of a pail of garbage dumped on his head without warning. Pigs and dogs—the informal municipal sanitation service —wandered about. (Medieval London was more finicky, decreeing that "he who will nourish a pig, let him keep it in his own house.")

But the daytime vitality of medieval streets was extraordinary! In Paris one might encounter:

The beggars who sat at the church doors and by the bridges, the peasants who came in from the country to buy and sell, the artisans and craftsmen in their open shops, the hawkers and merchants, jongleurs and mountebanks, monks and friars, canons of the cathedral and professors of the university, students and schoolboys; couriers with their white wands, heralds in tabards, knights in armour; nobles riding out to hawk or hunt outside the city, ladies taking the air in litters, judges in their scarlet riding to the Law Courts, pilgrims going to Ste. Geneviève, prisoners, gyved and bound, being driven to the Grand Châtelet; and, secure within his turreted fortifications, the King in the Louvre.[9]

In reaction to the disorder and clutter that characterized the late medieval city, military engineers and planners pushed aside its crooked walls and alleys, and built broad, straight avenues.[10] Winding, narrow city streets stymied the movement of wheeled traffic; avenues encouraged it, as did technical advances such as the replacement of the old-fashioned solid wheel with one built of separate parts, and the development of iron tire rims and springs.

Some rulers even believed that winding streets and dark alleys encouraged revolution. Napoleon III was well aware of the

This 1843 London street scene—a view of St. Paul's from Ludgate Hill—will seem familiar to any urban pedestrian. All the present-day elements are here: a dangerous and chaotic mix of wheel and foot, with pedestrians crowding each other on narrow sidewalks.

fervor of Parisians, having risen to power himself in the aftermath of the Revolution of 1848. On his orders Baron Haussmann, prefect of the capital area, cut boulevards through Paris, and in the process destroyed the warren of streets used by three generations of revolutionaries. As an example, the Boulevard Saint-Michel was

[20]

hacked through the heart of the ancient Latin Quarter. The boulevards also facilitated the rapid deployment of troops within the city.[11]

While ancient and medieval city streets were narrow and pedestrian-oriented, the Renaissance streets were wider. (Leonardo da Vinci urged, as a rough rule of thumb, that "the street be as wide as the height of the houses.") With the subsequent transformation of widened streets to broad, straight avenues came a hardening of division between street users: there were those who walked, and those who rode. Lewis Mumford writes:

The sidewalk awnings in old New York City show a concern for the pedestrian not found today. These shopkeepers wanted to provide the best possible ambience for potential customers; protection from sun and rain were practical expedients to encourage trade.

In the medieval town the upper classes and the lower classes had jostled together on the street, in the marketplace, as they did in the cathedral: the rich might ride on horseback, but they must wait for the poor man with his bundle or the blind beggar groping with his stick to get out of the way. Now, with the development of the wide avenue, the dissociation of the upper and lower classes achieves form in the city itself. The rich drive; the poor walk. The rich roll along the axis of the grand avenue; the poor are off-center, in the gutter; and eventually a special strip is provided for the ordinary pedestrian, the sidewalk.[12]

These class distinctions are imbedded in the English language. It is perhaps from this period that "pedestrian" came also to mean humble, plodding, commonplace, lowly.

The fast-moving horse-drawn carriage did not, however, significantly alter city dimensions, based on footpower since Mesopotamian times. The revolutionary change took place in the nineteenth century, with the arrival, in rapid succession, of the cheap stagecoach, the railroad and the street trolley. For the first time, inexpensive transportation, other than footpower, became available to all classes. No longer would walking distances set limits on city growth.

These events coincided with a period when, as Lewis Mumford writes, the city was treated not as a public institution, but as a private commercial venture, to be

In the early 1900s, New York City Mayor William J. Gaynor, accompanied by his entourage, crossed the Brooklyn Bridge daily from his home to City Hall. A reminder of a time when even the mighty were pedestrians.

carved up in any fashion that might further the rise in land values. He continues:

Waterfronts might be made inaccessible to the stroller, ancient trees might be slaughtered and venerable buildings torn down to speed traffic.... No serious public recognition of the need for children's playgrounds came till after 1870, by which time the space needed could be acquired only at a colossal outlay. Hence the peculiar function of the over-developed street in the commercial plan: it was forced to take the place of the back garden and pro-

tected square of the medieval town, or of the open place and park of the baroque order. Thus this paved desert, adapted primarily to wheeled traffic, became also park, promenade, and playground: a grim park, a dusty promenade, a dangerous playground.[13]

Unremittingly, the street assumed its present condition: overburdened and overwhelmed. While many nineteenth-century residential streets remained tree-shaded and free of noise and confusion, downtown streets settled into a state of permanent chaos. Trolleys and a great variety of horse-drawn vehicles flooded even the widest of avenues. Of the congestion caused by horse-drawn vehicles, a Londoner wrote in 1890:

But the mud! [A euphemism] And the noise! And the smell! All these blemishes where [the] mark of the horse. ... London's crowded wheeled traffic ... was dense beyond movement. ... The deafening, side-drum tatoo of tyred wheels. ... It was an immensity of sound.[14]

Salvation lay with the automobile. Clean and quiet, occupying less space than the horse and wagon, carrying double or treble the load, moving faster, surely it would bring an end to urban congestion. The automobile's arrival was greeted with ecstasy. Few could then imagine the baleful effect it would have on city life!

But the automobile stole the street.

Man, beast and vehicle converge on Chicago's Dearborn Street—a 1910 example of vehicular and pedestrian demands hopelessly overloading the gridiron street system.

Today the street serves this single basic function: passageway and storage area for motor vehicles. No longer is it a place for human exchange and artistic enterprise.

The pedestrian of the past was better off than the pedestrian today. Caesar's daytime ban of cart and chariot traffic in Rome shows a concern for pedestrian welfare, even though his action may have created a city of insomniacs. Few public officials now even think about pedestrians.

The social life and activity found in the streets of classical Athens, fourth-century Antioch and the medieval city are rarely found in modern cities; we are the poorer for this. Street paving is no longer an art; seldom does street planning reflect a concern for beauty. For most of those who live in cities, the quiet tree-lined residential street is only a memory.

Through a more sensible management of the automobile, pedestrianism aims to restore the historic function and quality of city streets.

CHAPTER III
URBAN PEDESTRIAN ISLANDS

Pedestrian islands and *pedestrian districts* are ways to recapture urban open spaces for human use. Both place limits on the movement of conventional vehicles within their boundaries.

Pedestrian islands put existing street space to new uses. Sidewalk and roadbed changes, and the addition of landscaping, benches and pedestrian-scale street furniture, can revolutionize the urban scene. Pedestrian islands are not costly to create, since the space they occupy—the street itself—is already public property.

In this chapter, we examine proposals for pedestrian islands. Pedestrian districts, areas of pedestrian activity extending beyond the confines of the existing street system, are considered in Chapter IV. Many of the proposals we discuss in both chapters relate to New York City, but the

Park Avenue at 50th Street around 1922. The generous mall was destroyed to provide more space for cars.

Park Avenue at 50th Street today. Try to find the "park."

basic concepts are applicable to any city.

Widened Sidewalks

For the pedestrian, widened sidewalks would be a boon, reversing the decades-old policy of narrowing sidewalks to accommodate the motor vehicle. Several important avenues in New York City lend themselves to an immediate, simple and dramatic demonstration of how to recapture sidewalk space for the pedestrian. Streets in other cities offer similar opportunities.

The "park" on Manhattan's Park Avenue—islands of green in the middle of

eight lanes of traffic—provides the pedestrian with not much more than a place of refuge between lights. During this interlude, the stranded walker is free, if he chooses, to gaze upon the nearby planting bed. At the next change of light, he bounds off on the second lap of his trip across the avenue, perhaps refreshed by his momentary contact with nature. A more productive use of this space seems possible.

If these twenty-foot-wide planting beds were removed, and the space they occupied were added to one of the present fifteen-foot Park Avenue sidewalks, the result would be a major promenade thirty-

five feet wide, with no reduction in the traffic capacity of the street. A Park Avenue promenade running from 48th to 57th streets, in the heart of congested midtown Manhattan, would do much to improve the intolerable pedestrian conditions in that area. The Penn Central Railroad vents, now located on the mid-avenue islands, could be shifted to the widened sidewalk without difficulty.

Rows of trees could be planted along the Park Avenue promenade far enough away from the curb to avoid bumps by cars or damage from fumes and vibrations. The tree-starved avenue would begin to live up to its name! Office workers and evening strollers could relax on benches located on the promenade.

The widened sidewalk could be placed on either side of Park Avenue. Placing it on the western side has certain advantages. Since Park Avenue runs north-east, not due north, the west side of the avenue receives more total hours of sunlight during the year than the east side. Yet, in the summer, the west sidewalk is in the shade in the late afternoon, when the sun is at its hottest.

The same basic concept can be applied to Central Park South, an east-west avenue at 59th Street, running from Fifth Avenue to Columbus Circle at Broadway. On the downtown side of the street, the sidewalk is a mere fourteen feet, although major

hotels, such as the Plaza, as well as high apartment houses crowd along this stretch. The sidewalk not only leaves little room for pedestrians but also is completely out of scale with the imposing structures which rise from it. With some narrowing of the 59th Street roadbed, the walking area on the much-traveled building side could be widened, transforming Central Park South into a major promenade.

A stretch of Broadway, from 60th to 64th streets, also lends itself to sidewalk widening. A few benches now perilously cling to each end of a strip running down the center of the avenue. But with cars zooming by on both sides, only feet away, the area has all the tranquility of a battle zone. Were the litter-strewn, unused strip eliminated, and the space thus freed shifted to the west side of Broadway, the widened sidewalk would create a pedestrian walkway from Columbus Circle to the Lincoln Center for the Performing Arts at 64th Street. With a buffer of trees and shrubs affording protection from motor vehicles, and benches along the way, pedestrians could travel this stretch in safety, comfort and style.

The cumulative effect of these sidewalk-widening links would be to create a mile-long promenade running along Park Avenue from 48th to 57th streets, then continuing at Fifth Avenue and 59th Street, along Central Park South to Co-

Park Avenue as a pedestrian way looking south toward Grand Central Station. The planting strip has been lifted from the center of the avenue and added to the sidewalk. The widened sidewalk has ample space for benches and trees. The lighting is human-scale, and paving stones provide variety underfoot. (Pomerance & Breines, Architects)

Central Park South could also become a pedestrian way by narrowing the 59th Street roadbed which runs parallel to the southern boundary of Central Park. (Pomerance & Breines, Architects)

Broadway as a pedestrian way looking south toward Columbus Circle. Here, as with Park Avenue, the planting strip has been lifted from the center of the avenue and added to the sidewalk. Another candidate for similar treatment in Manhattan is Lenox Avenue, running from 110th Street to 145th Street. (Pomerance & Breines, Architects)

lumbus Circle, and up Broadway to Lincoln Center. Visually, the promenade would enhance the cityscape. Socially, it would provide agreeable strolling condi-tions, and by so doing, enrich the urban residents' life.

Park Streets

Traffic congestion and pollution are noticeably more visible in downtown business areas, but the automobile has not left residential districts unscarred. Pedestrian islands, which would help so much in congested business areas, make good sense in the home environment as well. Park streets are an application of the pedestrian concept to residential areas of the city.

An eighteenth-century traveler to New York City observed: "In the chief streets there are trees planted, which in summer give them a fine appearance, and during the excessive heat at that time, afford a cooling shade. I found it extremely pleasant to walk in the town for it seemed quite like a garden."

Few streets now fit this description. Our residential streets were designed for another age. Their present role, as an automobile storage area, is an alien use. At the time the street system was laid out, in the horse era, parking posed no serious problem. When not in use, horse and buggy were retired to a stable, not left abandoned in the street. The automobile has proven to be less accommodating. The curb is its stable. Cars disfigure block after block. Traffic in motion and the parked vehicle are the most dominant, visible factors on the urban scene.

So pervasive is the tyranny of the automobile that closing a single block to traffic

Hammarskjöld Plaza near the United Nations is an example of an existing widened sidewalk.

East 8th Street on Manhattan's Lower East Side shares the fate of many urban residential streets. The automobile has taken over the roadway and destroyed the sidewalk. The pedestrian is hemmed in by cars. The sense of the street as an open public space is gone.

becomes a complex procedure. In New York City a play street, from which traffic and parking are excluded, cannot be authorized without a commitment by two adults to supervise the street. (The irony of it—a deadly threat to children will only be banned from the street if adult supervisors are present!) Even with adult supervision, a play street is not permitted if the block has nearby recreational facilities, or if any commercial establishment is located on it. When these conditions are met, a play street can operate only during the summer months. From October through May, eight months of the year, they are banned![1]

Park streets could alter today's dismal residential street scene. Closed to parking and through traffic, except for service and emergency vehicles, a park street can be

as short as one block, or several blocks in length. Sidewalk curbs would be removed and the roadbed filled in, thus turning the entire street, from building to building, into a pedestrian area. Decorative pavement would replace asphalt, and trees would be planted in the former roadbed. Here the trees could grow free from the damage of trucks and parking cars that trees planted three feet or less from the curb suffer. Appropriate street furniture and pedestrian-scale lighting would be introduced.

Children and cars are a lethal mix.

East 8th Street as a park street. This drawing is made directly from the above photograph, with no change in the buildings except for the modernized storefronts. The character of the street, however, has radically changed. On a park street, the chief pedestrian victims of the automobile—the young and the elderly—have nothing to fear. (Pomerance & Breines, Architects; M. Paul Friedberg & Associates, Landscape Architects)

Eliminating vehicular traffic from streets where young children play will relieve parents of constant anxiety over their safety.

Park streets will delight children. Over the years the automobile has encroached more and more on children's play space. Even after Old Dobbin was declared extinct, streets remained traffic-free much of the time, providing a play area at one's very doorstep. This changed as car ownership became more widespread.

Two streets—8th and 9th, between Avenues A and C on New York City's Lower East Side, provide a microcosm of the change. As late as 1950, these streets were still prime ball-game and roller-skating areas. As the automobile gained ascendancy in the 1950s, through traffic increased and the curbside became a parking lot. With the loss of the street as a play area, children began to spill over to the nearest available open space, which happened to be the formal lawns and planting of Riis Houses, with their English-style landscaping. The invasion of this space, never designed for play use, set off a ruckus between the children and the managers of Riis Houses, a public-housing project named for Jacob Riis, the journalist crusader for improved social conditions, and author of *How the Other Half Lives.*

At this point, as the dispute became in-

Cars owned by 8th Street residents could be placed in a garage built on an existing empty lot. The garage shown is a half-level below the street, partially covered by a sitting deck. Vehicle entry would be from the adjoining street. (Pomerance & Breines, Architects; M. Paul Friedberg & Associates, Landscape Architects)

creasingly acrimonious, the New York City Housing Authority appealed to the Vincent Astor Foundation, which in turn retained Pomerance and Breines, Architects, and Paul Friedberg Associates, Landscape Architects, to find a solution. Riis Houses Plaza, a three-acre pedestrian area and playground which replaced a portion of the formal lawns, provided a partial answer. But even this was not sufficient to compensate for the lost street space. Accordingly, the proposed Riis-Tompkins Park Street was an effort, unfortunately never realized, to recapture this traditional open-space area for the residents of 8th and 9th streets.

The convenience of park streets will benefit adults too, especially elderly people. The aged, like children, are at the mercy of convenience. With cleaner air,

Riis Houses with its formal lawns and plantings.

trees and a place to relax only a few feet away, less time need be spent sitting indoors, often alone.

Traditionally, streets have served as a communal outdoor living room. The automobile destroyed the age-old amenities of the pedestrian realm. Park streets will restore them. Streets will again be an integral part of home and community life. "Lowly, unpurposeful and random as they may appear, sidewalk contacts," Jane

The same three acres, but put to far more productive use. There is a garden walk for adults in the foreground, a playground for children in the distance and an amphitheater for everyone in the center. (Pomerance & Breines, Architects; Paul Friedberg Associates, Landscape Architects)

Jacobs has written, "are the small change from which a city's wealth of public life may grow."[2]

The New York City metropolitan area, along with most urban centers, suffers from a severe shortage of recreation space. For example, Queens, a borough of New York City, needs 32,000 more acres of parkland to meet the standards set for open space by the National Recreation Association.[3] Streets comprise about one third of the total land in cities, with street space far exceeding parks and beaches as the primary source of open space in the city. Residential streets are an unexploited open-space resource lying at our very feet.

Of the seventy-four communities comprising New York City, nine have 53 percent of the recreational acreage. This unfair geographical distribution is not unique to New York City. Park streets can help ease the problem. Unlike the usual recreational area, to which few neighborhoods have convenient access, streets are evenly distributed throughout a city.

Park streets can fill an important need by providing green breathing spaces in high density residential areas. They are economical. The purchase cost of a vest-pocket park in New York City averages $300,000 per acre. No land purchase funds are needed for park streets, since they reclaim public land for the public.

What is to be done about cars denied

access to park streets? Allowing for fire hydrants, curb cuts and occasional bus stops, the average residential city block has parking space for about fifteen cars along each curb, or thirty cars in all. In most cases, these few spaces are not sufficient for all the automobiles owned by residents. Only a lucky or resourceful few manage to get to the curb on time. This means that entire streets are despoiled for the convenience of a small number of car owners, whose cars sit at the curb on the average of twenty-two hours each day.[4]

If custom has established certain parking rights, the municipality may wish to assume the burden of providing alternate parking facilities to free the street for its more socially valuable role as a pedestrian island. The Riis-Tompkins Park Street design suggests one way to provide such off-street parking where vacant lots exist along the proposed park street. By locating the parking at a half-level below the street, a public sitting area can be achieved over part of the space, thereby enhancing the street even further.

Where such an off-street facility is not possible, a garage may be required at another location. This could involve added expense and inconvenience to car owners. But the decision on whether or not to create a park street is one all the residents

Every revolution has its street barricades. If made off-limits to the automobile, residential streets are a natural play space for children.

of the street—both those who do and those who don't own cars—should be allowed to make. Park streets should not be foisted on anyone. In fact, after the municipality has completed its work in making the street over, the park street will need lots of tender loving care from the people who live on it. Only blocks where appreciable numbers of people want and will enjoy the benefits of a park street should get them.

Twenty years ago Frank Lloyd Wright said of New York City, "You'll see more greenery in twenty-five years. Grass will grow where least expected now and flowers will bloom in the concrete." With park streets, his prophecy can be realized in all cities.

Pedestrian Islands in Downtown Business Areas

Three things are needed to create a part-time pedestrian island in a downtown

business area, or anywhere else: imagination, the will to achieve it and a traffic barrier.

Nassau Street is the most successful part-time street-closing in New York City. Along with Wall Street and Broadway—neighboring streets in the financial district —Nassau is one of the city's oldest thoroughfares. Today it struggles to carry modern traffic, pedestrian and vehicular, on rights of way laid out when the city was a tiny center in an agrarian economy depending on transportation little improved since the Middle Ages—that is, except from 11 A.M. to 2 P.M. each weekday, for since the spring of 1969, a five-block stretch of Nassau Street has been declared a vehicle-free pedestrian island.

Prior to the street-closing, nine thousand pedestrians an hour jammed into the five-block area at midday and fought for the honor of occupying space on the narrow ten-foot sidewalks. The former cow path was overrun by a two-footed herd. Lunch hour was a grim confrontation between man and machine. Man, fragile and easy to dent, did not fare well in the competition.

Nothing more formidable or expensive than a traffic sign placed in the middle of the roadbed reading "STREET CLOSED, 11 A.M.-2 P.M., MON THRU FRI" has revolutionized Nassau Street. Stepping off the

Sidewalk rip-off in Rome.

STREETS WITHOUT CARS

curb at the wrong moment is no longer as dangerous as stepping off a cliff. Many more pedestrians than before can now walk in comfort and safety. Nassau Street pedestrians delight in their roadbed triumph. In this regard, they are less awed by the automobile than their pedestrian counterparts in Milan, who keep to the sidewalk and remain apprehensive about walking in the roadbed, so long a no man's land, even on streets closed to traffic for their special use.

Placed end to end, New York City's 6,123 miles of street would reach from New York to Moscow and part of the way back. Many of these streets are not needed for vehicular use twenty-four hours a day, 365 days a year. Increasing the number of part-time pedestrian streets will make any city a more pleasant place to live.*

Part-time pedestrian islands can mitigate the effects of downtown congestion

---

* Wall Street is an excellent candidate for a part-time pedestrian street. If the 480,000 people working in the Wall Street financial district ever simultaneously issued forth from their offices, the narrow sidewalks would be covered with a layer of humanity one and one-half people thick.

New York's Nassau Street: urban insanity (left) and a pedestrianized version (right).

by closing streets to motor vehicles during periods of most intensive use. Full-time pedestrian islands, however, are often a more satisfactory solution.

A full-time pedestrian island is an area where the existing street has been redesigned for pedestrian use, not merely closed to traffic, and where vehicles are excluded for most of the day. Some full-time pedestrian islands ban all motor vehicles, others ban certain types of vehicles.

A full-time pedestrian island may evolve from a part-time island which has proven to be a success. The ease and the economy with which a street can be temporarily closed encourage experimentation. This opportunity to experiment is unique to pedestrian engineering.

Nicollet Mall in Minneapolis. Nicollet Avenue formerly was host to 12,000 vehicles a day. Now landscaping and heated bus shelters are among the pedestrian amenities.

Unlike most plans to improve urban life, which often are so vast as to preclude implementation, planning for pedestrians can be undertaken experimentally and in stages.

Copenhagen's Strøget provides an example of this process. What started as a three-month street-closing experiment was extended for an additional twelve-month test. Strøget is now a permanent pedestrian haven and one of the smartest shopping streets in Europe. The street is a little over a mile in length, varying in width from thirty feet for most of the distance to one hundred feet at certain points. Following the successful experimental phase, it was repaved, with a dark center strip to demarcate the vehicle-bearing lane. (Emergency vehicles can enter Strøget at any time; other vehicles from 4 A.M. to 11 A.M.)

Nassau Street is also on the way to becoming a full-time pedestrian island. Proposals for the elimination of the roadbed and repaving of the street are under consideration. The second stage in its pedestrian development might never have been reached had not part-time closings established the value of a pedestrian island in this crowded section of New York City.

The best-known full-time pedestrian island in the United States is the Nicollet Mall in Minneapolis, Minnesota. It has been described as the most important

Planted less than two feet from the curb, this tree and its faithful tulip have a short life expectancy. Their deadly enemies? Car fenders and vehicular pollution.

American piece of urban design in the last thirty years. The mall covers an eight-block section containing the city's major retail stores. Prior to its completion in 1968, twelve thousand vehicles, largely private cars, entered this stretch of Nicollet Avenue each day, mingling with tens of thousands of pedestrians, not a few of whom were mangled in the process.[5]

Today two traffic lanes, serpentine in design, remain in operation. Buses, taxis and emergency vehicles may drive along them; automobiles may not. The balance of the street has been redesigned for pedestrian use. To encourage such activity, the sidewalks have been widened, and benches, street sculpture, pedestrian-scale lighting, and landscaping placed along them. Pavements with snow-melting capability are in use.

From the outset, downtown Minneapolis retailers saw the mall as a means to stem the loss of customers to suburban shopping centers. At the retailers' urging, the Minnesota State Legislature created a mall assessment district. Construction and maintenance costs for the enterprise have been met largely from assessments levied against these retailers. The success of the Nicollet Mall has exceeded all expectations, serving as a key factor in the revival of downtown Minneapolis. It has proven to the public, especially to merchants, that restraining the automobile can be good for business.

These trees, planted well back from the street curb on a widened sidewalk, are safe from vehicular harm and will thrive.

THE PEDESTRIAN REVOLUTION

New York City's Madison Avenue, from 44th to 57th streets, seems ideal territory for a mall. The avenue is bedlam. (John Steinbeck, in his tripartite swipe at New York City, may have had this area in mind when he said, "Its climate is a scandal, its politics are used to frighten children, its traffic is madness.") The sidewalks, designed originally for residential use, pared down to speed traffic flow and now supporting office buildings and high-quality retail stores, are awash with humanity. Open space in the area is at a premium.

Studies reveal that closing Madison Avenue to motor vehicles, other than buses, would divert only 3 percent of all motor-vehicle traffic in the central square mile of mid-Manhattan, involving some 20,000 trips by motorists. Two hundred thousand pedestrian trips a day along the avenue would benefit directly, and another 600,000 on crosstown streets indirectly, because the avenue could now be crossed with greater ease. An additional 20,000 pedestrian trips would be attracted to Madison Avenue if the traffic congestion were eliminated.[6]

Madison Avenue in New York City, looking north from 51st Street. Many people never leave their offices at all during lunchtime to avoid traffic-jammed streets and crowds along the avenue's narrow thirteen-foot sidewalks; retailers suffer accordingly.

The Madison Mall. Most midday trips in midtown Manhattan are by foot. The Madison Mall could have provided a delightful, relaxed setting for tens of thousands of strollers and shoppers in this high-density area. (Don C. Miles, Office of Midtown Planning and Development, Designer)

A pedestrian island, based on the Nicollet model except that taxis would also be banned, was therefore proposed for this section of Madison Avenue by Mayor John V. Lindsay in 1971. But the taxi interests opposed it, since the mall would have denied them access to a lucrative cruising area, and the retail community was divided over the proposal. This com-

bined opposition led to rejection of the mall by a New York City governing body, the Board of Estimate.

In defeat, the Madison Mall provides several useful lessons for pedestrian advocates. First of all, Mayor Lindsay made the mistake of announcing plans for a permanent Madison Mall without involving the taxi industry and retailers in the planning process. Had the mall initially been proposed as an experiment, following planning sessions with these groups and with others, it might have gained, if not their enthusiastic support, at least their less strident opposition. He then sought to by-pass the Board of Estimate, contending that action by that body was not legally required. Challenged in court on this point, he lost. By this time, the opposition of the taxi industry, merchants and the Board of Estimate was assured.

To try to salvage something from the wreckage, the proposal was scaled down from a permanent mall to a ninety-day experiment. To many people, however, the experimental aspect appeared to be more a ploy to obtain Board of Estimate approval than a commitment to evaluate the results of the experiment impartially. In addition, the Madison Mall proposal may have been too ambitious a pedestrian plan for a city where, with the exception of Nassau Street, pedestrian engineering is still at an early stage. The midtown Man-

hattan area can benefit enormously from pedestrianism, but also presents some of the most difficult traffic diversion problems. Modest, and successful, experiments elsewhere in the city might have built up public and political support, as well as a body of valuable experience, for this much more major undertaking.

Proposals for pedestrian areas are no different than any planning proposal: those persons most affected expect to be consulted and shown that the proposal can work. Pedestrian engineering, with its emphasis on experimentation, encourages close consultation during both the planning and the experimental stages. As people are brought into the planning and the realization of the experiment, they become educated in the process. To paraphrase Marshall MacLuhan, the author and communications theorist—the experiment is the message.

The Karlsplatz/Marienplatz pedestrian island in the heart of Munich's shopping and entertainment center is an example of a pedestrian area developing with strong public support. Citizens worked to obtain city council approval for the project, and were consulted on the architectural design of the mall through a newspaper poll.[7]

Merchant opposition to pedestrian areas should not be deemed a foregone conclusion. The Minneapolis merchants who work for, *and paid for,* the Nicollet Mall,

are ample proof of this. But one cannot ignore the fact that merchants are often in the forefront of opposition to pedestrian-area proposals.

Several considerations may help to ease merchant fears:

1. A pedestrian area begins as an experiment. If the experiment does not work —and its effect on business will be an important factor in evaluating the results—it should be discontinued.

2. People in cars do not buy goods; people on foot do.

3. In confirmation of the prior statement, merchants with stores in pedestrian areas benefit from increased sales. On Copenhagen's Strøget, for example, the merchants, who initially opposed closing the street to vehicles, report sales increases of 25 to 40 percent.[8] Similar results are reported from cities as diverse as Vienna, Tokyo, Minneapolis and Munich.

4. Pedestrian islands are open to emergency vehicles at all times, and to delivery trucks at certain hours each day.

5. The carnival atmosphere of some pedestrian areas—such as volley-ball games outside Tiffany's Fifth Avenue jewelry store—which merchants believe discourage sales, will vanish as pedestrianism becomes a regular part of daily life rather than a holiday event.

Two historical notes may be relevant at this point. First, Rockefeller Center, with its street-level mall and underground concourse, is one of New York City's great success stories. It has been a major stabilizing force for retailers and property owners along Fifth Avenue. Yet when Rockefeller Center was conceived over forty years ago, it was opposed by Fifth Avenue merchants and property owners, who feared its competition. If the decision had been theirs, Rockefeller Center would never have been built. Second, the Florentine gold and silver smiths who have their shops on the Ponte Vecchio, spanning the Arno River, petitioned the city authorities a few years ago to end the ban of many hundred years against vehicle use on the bridge. The mayor of Florence rejected the request, commenting, "Florence's merchants were intelligent in the fifteenth century, but they do not seem to have maintained the level."

Moral: Merchants are not always the best judges of their own, or the public's, interest.

With any proposal to create a pedestrian island in a downtown business area, an inevitable question arises: Will the diverted vehicles bring traffic to a standstill elsewhere?

Some peripheral congestion is inevitable at first. The congestion will ease as drivers adjust to the diversion routes and a drop in traffic occurs. The traffic drop-

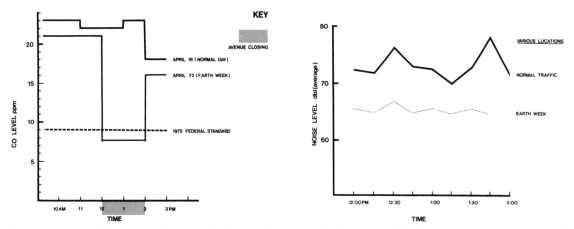

Carbon-monoxide and noise levels dropped dramatically when Madison Avenue was closed to cars at midday during Earth Week in 1971. Carbon-monoxide levels, in fact, dropped from a normal 22 parts per million to about 7—two parts per million better than the 1975 federal air-quality standard. (Sources: New York City Office of Midtown Planning and Development, and Department of Air Resources)

off is the result of an interesting phenomenon operating in reverse. Just as additional vehicular facilities generate more traffic, reducing opportunities for vehicle use diminishes traffic. This happens when, for convenience' sake, some motorists shift to other, more efficient means of transportation. Thus, when Copenhagen's Strøget, a once heavily traveled street, was closed to motor vehicles, only 30 percent of its peak-hour traffic was traced to neighboring streets.[9]

This short-term congestion, and the inconvenience to people who decide to alter their mode of transportation, must be balanced against the benefits of a pedestrian island: in the case of the proposed Madison Mall, improved conditions for

hundreds of thousands of pedestrian users versus 20,000 motorists inconvenienced. Hardly a delicate balance by any weighing of benefits.

Pedestrian engineering—a gradual planning process involving close consultation with those persons most likely to be affected, and subject to review and evaluation at each stage of the experiment—can help to ensure the orderly reduction of road space.

Vehicular traffic will be further reduced as more and more people come to enjoy their car-free pedestrian island, with convenient access to work and to shops, and as they recognize, as Henry James did a century ago, that there is no better way of taking in life than walking in the street.

CHAPTER IV
URBAN PEDESTRIAN DISTRICTS

Pedestrian islands, described in the previous chapter, put existing street space to new uses. *Pedestrian districts,* not limited to present street patterns, create entirely new walking areas. Footpower meets most transportation needs of a pedestrian island, since islands cover a relatively small area. Some pedestrian districts are larger in size. These will require a form of transportation less powerful than a conventional vehicle to supplement footpower. Mini-vehicle is the name we give to this supplementary transport. Examples of

Midtown Manhattan encompasses one of the most intensive agglomerations of human activity in the world. Yet, as a report of the Office of Midtown Planning and Development indicates, "It is noticeably lacking in the kinds of periodic open spaces which provide trees and other greenery and relief from the intensity of activity—oases which allow the visitor, shopper, and office worker to pause, collect his wits, relax his feet, or chat with a friend." Bryant Park is one of the few existing oases in the area.

Americans are supposed to be a people on the move. If benches and sitting areas were provided in the business sections of our cities, would we even stop to use them? Rockefeller Plaza in New York City conclusively answered this question a half-century ago.

mini-vehicles are bicycles and electric-powered tractor-trains. Pedestrian districts are discussed in this chapter, and different types of mini-vehicles in chapters V and VI.

Grand Central Terminal in New York City, built in 1913, is a pedestrian district. This may surprise the reader who thinks of a pedestrian district as a new-fangled concept; yet only pedestrians have access to Grand Central's thirty acres and several levels. Its pedestrian network links together railroad and subway connections, office buildings and hotels. Viaducts out-side Grand Central divert conventional traffic past the station. Inside, Grand Central has its own mini-vehicle system to transport luggage, mail and supplies. Hundreds of thousands of people circulate through this pedestrian district each day without the disrupting effect of conventional vehicles.

More recent examples of pedestrian districts in the United States are L'Enfant Plaza in downtown Washington, D.C., a pedestrian complex comprising commercial and government buildings, hotels and shops; the Prudential Center in Boston,

where a hotel, an office building and apartment houses are linked by extensive plazas and shop-lined concourses; and Investors Diversified Services (IDS) Center in Minneapolis, consisting of a fifty-one-story office tower, a nineteen-story hotel, shops and another office building, all arranged around a central glass-roofed court.

Thru-Block Walkways

Comparing European to American streets on his first visit to the United States, Jean-Paul Sartre wrote: "Ours are oblique and twisting, full of bends and secrets. The American street is a straight line that gives itself away immediately. It contains no mystery." Sartre, of course, is referring to the familiar gridiron street pattern so conspicuous in the United States.

The gridiron pattern was imposed on New York City as early as 1811. Hundreds of miles of street north of 14th Street were laid out in gridiron fashion, to avoid repetition in undeveloped sections of the tangled street maze of the older parts of the city. The hills, woods, and streams of Manhattan lying in the path of the draftsman's unrelenting straight lines were removed. Tradition has it that a member of the commission created by the New York State Legislature to make the street-extension plan, weary of the long discussions, picked up a mason's wire screen, placed it on the large map of Manhattan lying on the table and said, "Here is a plan. Let the larger, vertical wires represent the north and south avenues, and the frequent small cross wires the streets that go east and west," and without further ado, the plan was adopted.[1]

Yet it would be a mistake to conclude that the United States is the original source of gridiron planning. Lewis Mumford writes:

The only fact that makes it more conspicuous in America than in the old world is the ab-

The Graduate Center of the City University of New York. This mid-block passage between Fifth and Sixth avenues could serve as a link in 5½ Way. Light-washed textures of concrete and a gently ramped bluestone floor, writes *New York Times* architectural critic Ada Louise Huxtable, invite the pedestrian to enjoy the rugged elegance of this passageway—a welcome respite from the surrounding honky-tonk of the Times Square area. (Carl J. Petrilli, Architect)

THE PEDESTRIAN REVOLUTION

Street-Level Improvements in Midtown Area

Zoning incentives have encouraged developers to build numerous plazas and arcades, but, as this map of midtown Manhattan shows, these street-level improvements bear no relationship to one another. Each has been built to suit the convenience of a particular developer. Were the zoning incentive part of an overall plan for the area, the open spaces could be linked together, as thru-block walkways or sections in a strollway system.

sence, except for areas like the original settlements of Boston and New York, of earlier types of city planning. From the seventeenth century onward, Western city extensions, as in Stuttgart and Berlin, in London and Edinburgh, were made in the same fashion, except where ancient water courses, roads, or field boundaries had established lines that could not be lightly over-ridden. The beauty of this new mechanical pattern, from a commercial standpoint, should be plain. ... Such plans fitted nothing but a quick parcelling of the land, a

quick conversion of farmsteads into real estate, and a quick sale.[2]

Thru-block walkways break out of the centuries-old gridiron strait jacket. They are pedestrian districts which run between avenues, threading their way through the middle of existing blocks.

Fifth Avenue marks the boundary between Manhattan's East Side and West Side. East of Fifth Avenue, the first few blocks vary between 400 and 420 feet in length. West of Fifth Avenue, the first three blocks, in most places, are 800 feet long. Jane Jacobs describes the adventures of a plucky would-be west-of-Fifth-Avenue thru-block walker.

A reporter for *The New Yorker,* observing that people *try* to find an extra north-south passage in the too-long blocks between Fifth and Sixth Avenues, once attempted to see if he could amalgamate a makeshift mid-block trail from Thirty-third Street to Rockefeller Center. He discovered reasonable, if erratic, means for short-cutting through nine of the blocks, owing to block-through stores and lobbies and Bryant Park behind the Forty-second Street Library. But he was reduced to wiggling under fences or clambering through windows or coaxing superintendents, to get through four of the blocks, and had to evade the issue by going into subway passages for two.[3]

This very area is one of New York City's most congested trouble spots. The sidewalks of both Fifth Avenue and Sixth Av-

STREETS WITHOUT CARS

enue, known also as the Avenue of the Americas, teem with office workers, while heavy traffic rumbles along the roadbed. Walking space is in short supply, and attractive pedestrian areas are nonexistent except for Bryant Park, located between 40th and 42nd streets on Sixth Avenue, and Rockefeller Center.

A thru-block walkway in midtown Manhattan could begin at Bryant Park,

Thru-block walkway behind Burlington House. Having no connection to other spaces located nearby, this delightful one-block passageway unfortunately ends at the first curb.

weave its way north through the long blocks between Fifth and Sixth avenues to Rockefeller Center, and then continue on to Central Park at 59th Street. When first introduced in 1964 by the architectural

Map of 5½ Way. The exact route will depend on the availability of land and whether development is along commercial or residential lines, or a mix of both. Shaded areas represent walkways and paths. (Pomerance & Breines, Architects)

firm of Pomerance and Breines, this proposal was dubbed "5½ Way."

Since a thru-block walkway serves pedestrians, it need not be straight in line or uniform in width. A walkway may be sinuous in form, narrow in one part, wider in another, and may pass through arcades.

Bryant Park is the southernmost link in 5½ Way. The next link, directly across 42nd Street, already exists. This is the

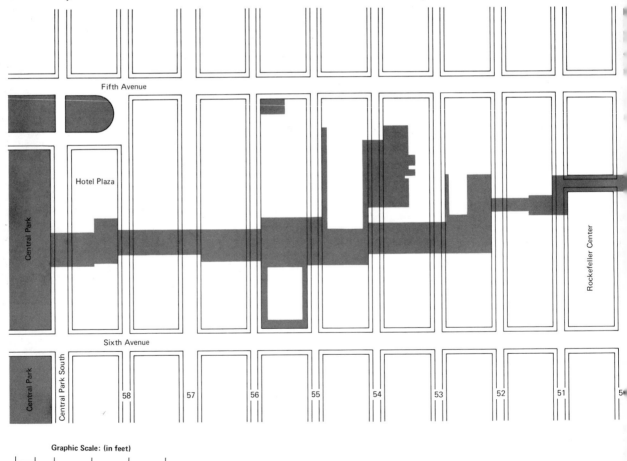

Fifth Avenue

Hotel Plaza

Central Park

Rockefeller Center

Central Park

Central Park South

Sixth Avenue

58   57   56   55   54   53   52   51   5

Graphic Scale: (in feet)

0   80   160   320   480   640

N

mid-block pedestrian arcade of the City University Graduate Center, which runs between 42nd and 43rd streets. The arcade provides 16,000 square feet of public pedestrian space in a mid-block passage 200 feet long.

Other possible links in 5½ Way, in addition to Rockefeller Plaza from 48th to 51st streets, are the thru-block arcades of the Tishman Building, between 52nd and

53rd streets, and the Squibb Building, between 56th and 57th streets.

By creating a north-south pedestrian avenue, 5½ Way would provide additional walking space in the area where the need for it is greatest, with no diminution of vehicle space. As some people shift to the new mid-block passage, pedestrian congestion along Fifth and Sixth avenues would lessen.

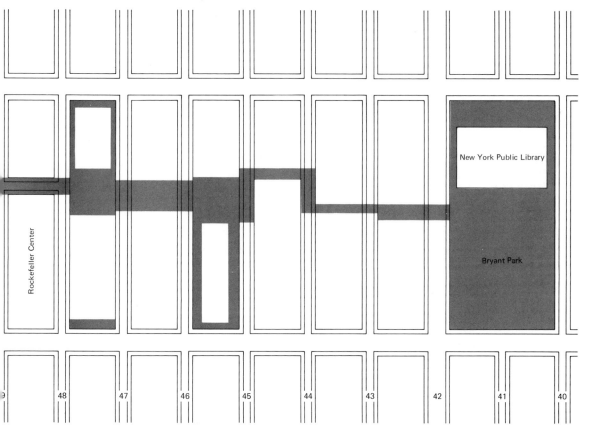

THE PEDESTRIAN REVOLUTION

Through imaginative zoning, 5½ Way can come into being. The 1961 revision of the New York City Zoning Ordinance was hailed as a pedestrian breakthrough because it discouraged the notorious wedding-cake office structures so prevalent under the old zoning. Those commercial structures would rise up eighty-five feet from the building line, the line at street level up to which a building can be built, and then break back in ziggurat fashion. The effect was to make dark canyons of the streets and avenues.

To encourage open public space at street level, the new zoning offers the office-building developer a bonus of up to an additional 20 percent in building floor area for the creation of plazas and arcades. (The bonus is also available for residential development in certain districts.) During the office construction boom of the 1960s, the bonus proved a powerful incentive to New York builders, as shown on the accompanying map of plazas and arcades built in midtown Manhattan.

But pedestrian expectations remain unrealized, for the developers and architects understandably placed the plazas and arcades wherever convenient on their property, with no relationship, however, to adjoining open spaces. Most plazas, isolated from each other, with few shops or restaurants at street level, fail to serve, let alone attract, the pedestrian. In the absence of a flow of people, some plazas and arcades have become maintenance and security headaches for their owners—hangouts for derelicts and a prey to vandals. Some planners, in their disappointment, have come full circle and now advocate the elimination of the bonus provision for plazas. This would be a mistake. Open plazas and arcades make sense; the failure has been in not making these open spaces part of a larger plan, or sufficiently inviting to attract pedestrians. On the latter point, New York City Mayor Abraham D. Beame has proposed amending the rules governing the bonus provision to encourage builders of future plazas to provide trees, benches, fountains and other pedestrian amenities.

5½ Way, and thru-block walkways in other sections of New York, and in other cities, can be achieved by conditioning the zoning bonus for plazas and arcades on conformance with an open space plan for the area developed by the municipal planning authorities. The plan would link the open spaces in a continuous chain of pedestrian walkways. In the case of 5½ Way, the area between Fifth and Sixth avenues from 42nd to 59th streets could be designated a 5½ Way Zoning District. As an incentive to developers, buildings along

View of 5½ Way. The concept of a thru-block walkway can be applied to any city. (Pomerance & Breines, Architects)

[54]

jacqueline Adato

this pedestrian avenue would be allowed the same development rights now available only to buildings on conventional avenues. High mid-block densities are feasible where traffic and vehicular pollution is absent. A pedestrian avenue such as 5½ Way would have neither. (This assumes that some side streets would be closed to traffic on a part- or full-time basis.) With no need for a roadbed along 5½ Way, generous amounts of open space would be available to pedestrians.

A walkway's open-space areas would remain in private ownership and be privately maintained, continuing to pay real estate taxes to the municipality, while serving as a public, pedestrian street. It would not cost a penny in public funds. In place of postage-stamp-sized plazas and scattered arcades, the city and its citizens will acquire a traffic-free connecting walkway. Shops and restaurants on 5½ Way would stimulate pedestrian activity, encouraging day and nighttime use of the thru-block walkway.

A proposal to develop 5½ Way as a residential project is discussed in Chapter IX, "The Pedestrian Advocate." This would provide thousands of New Yorkers with the opportunity to walk to work.

Underground Streets

A goal of pedestrian engineering is to reduce the dependence of cities on horse-power by encouraging and enlarging opportunities for footpower. Mass transit is important to achieve this goal. An improved mass-transportation system will serve to discourage private-car use in cities. This in turn enhances opportunities for pedestrianism.

Mass-transit systems in American cities have suffered sharp declines in ridership over the past decade. The Lexington Avenue line, New York's busiest subway route, experienced patronage losses amounting to nearly one passenger in seven at its East Side stations in Manhattan over the past decade. This decline is the equivalent of more than forty-five days' patronage on the route a decade ago.[4] Inhuman riding conditions are certainly a factor in the decline.

One way to enhance both systems, mass transit and pedestrian, is to create attractive pedestrian concourses—underground streets—at important subway points. Most New York City subway concourses are ugly, dirty and unsafe; an insult to the millions of riders forced to use them. Frank Lloyd Wright summed it all up when he was asked to contrast the New York City subway system to Moscow's. "Compared to the Moscow Metro," he said, "New York's subway is a sewer!"

Underground streets.
New York (top) Montreal (middle) Mexico City (bottom)

THE PEDESTRIAN REVOLUTION

The underground concourse network of Rockefeller Center, running from 47th Street to 53rd Street, between Fifth and Sixth avenues, should be more the rule than an oft-cited exception. At Rockefeller Center, which was built during the Depression, attention to walking starts below the surface, with a one-and-a-half-mile concourse system, continues with a mall at street level and reaches as high as sixty-nine stories on the landscaped rooftops.[5]

Since commercial buildings usually have basement levels, it is feasible, as Rockefeller Center has shown, to plan building connections with adjacent subway stations. Thus, office workers can have direct access from their buildings by elevator or escalator to concourses which lead to the station.

In addition to creating agreeable conditions for mass-transit users, the Rockefeller Center complex, with off-street access to subways, reduces pedestrian crowding at street level. This is also true of "Underground Atlanta" in Georgia, and the Place Ville Marie's network of underground streets in Montreal. Much to their credit, the New York City Planning Commission and Metropolitan Transportation Authority, in cooperation with a civic organization, the Municipal Art Society, are encouraging pedestrian ameni-

ties at stations of the proposed Second Avenue subway through new zoning legislation. At the major Thirty-fourth Street and Forty-eighth Street stations, in particular, new buildings related to the future underground pedestrian concourses are required to build their basements so that connections can be made when the Second Avenue line is in operation.

Where the separation of foot and wheel is vertical, that is, through a sub-surface concourse or by a raised mezzanine, the danger exists that the intended beneficiaries may stubbornly refuse to use it. Many pedestrians make no serious attempt to cooperate with architects! The most

careful planning must be undertaken to ensure that concourses meet the needs and convenience of people on foot.

The flow of pedestrian traffic will encourage the development of shops, restaurants and other services along underground streets. These facilities, in turn, will attract more people. In such circumstances, the subway trip will be enhanced through the varied and interesting approaches to the station.

At present, natural light and fresh air are unnecessarily denied to people who circulate below ground. Concourses can be planned around sunken plazas open to the

Tight squeeze.

Renovation of a subway station on the Lexington Avenue Line in New York City (above). The Transit Authority is making a laudable effort to improve the appearance of subway stations as part of the campaign to halt the steady decline in ridership. Legible signs, bright colors and serviceable materials are notable features of the new subway designs. Hunter College in Manhattan (top right) is known as the subway campus. Most of its 10,000 students travel on the Lexington Avenue Line, which has a station at 68th Street. A planned subway concourse will connect Hunter College buildings directly to the station. Street-level access to the subway will be by open-stair wells sheltered under sidewalk arcades. (Ulrich Frazen & Associates, Architects). While footpower and mini-vehicles make movement within pedestrian districts feasible, a good mass-transportation system is needed to bring people to the district. This fume-free, air-conditioned electric trolley (bottom right) can supplement a subway system, and may be the answer for cities with no such facilities. Boston has ordered 150 of them.

sky. These plazas will serve as windows to the underground street. The sunken winter ice-skating rink—outdoor summer café of Rockefeller Center—demonstrates the feasibility of opening sub-surface concourses to the sky.

The convenience and attractiveness of underground streets, together with other improvements of the subway system, will help lure travelers away from the automobile. Indeed, pedestrian engineering works best when it provides attractive alternatives, rather than simply banning cars by decree.

Work-Residence Districts

Until the nineteenth century, the major part of the population walked to work in most cities. This did not always mean that their work place was located in the neighborhood. Even where it was not, the worker seldom traveled by foot more than two or three miles to his job.[6] The trolley

Wall Street during working hours on a weekday.

car and railroad extended the urban scale, and the automobile further extended and diffused it. Once walking distances no longer set the limits of city growth, significant separation of work and residence became first a possibility and then the general rule. Today, according to United States Census figures, about 300,000 New Yorkers, only 9.5 percent of the city's 3.1 million employed residents, regularly walk from home to work. Nationally, the percentage is considerably lower.

The burdens of travel weigh on both those who commute to the city from the suburbs and those who travel long distances to work from within the city. The journey to work is physically taxing, expensive and time-consuming. Assuming a trip of one hour each way—a modest trip for many people—exclusive of weekends and vacation, the time spent in transit each year is equal to all the traveler's waking hours in February.

The impact of these trips weighs heavily on each family. It takes its toll in rushed or missed meals, less leisure time for recreation and relaxation, and fewer opportunities to participate in the civic life of one's community. The zest of a new day is worn off before it has begun.

A World War II poster in Britain asked: "Is Your Journey Really Necessary?" Numerous journeys today would not be, if urban growth were rational. The wide

separation of work from residence forces many more people to travel than want to.

A work-residence pedestrian district, an area where opportunities for both work and residence are within walking distance or mini-vehicle range, can transform com-

Wall Street the rest of the time. By encouraging work-residence districts and strolling opportunities for city residents and visitors, pedestrian engineering would bring life to this area in the evening and on weekends.

muting from an endurance test to a delightful experience. The aim here is not to reduce mobility, only wasteful movement.

Industrial, commercial and residential uses are often incompatible, but they need not be as rigidly segregated as they are today. As city economies continue their movement away from industry to service and office activity, use incompatibility will become even less of a problem.

Wall Street is an example of a single-use district. It functions for less than half a day on weekdays, from 8:30 A.M. to 5:30 P.M., and not at all on weekends—a phenomenally inefficient use of urban space. So desolate is Wall Street on weekends that Norman Mailer, the author and a New York City mayoral candidate in 1969, proposed that the financial district's concrete canyons be used as the site of the stickball world series.

But in lower Manhattan, as elsewhere, pedestrianism is now on the march. Two major projects, Battery Park City and Manhattan Landing, will bring round-the-clock activity to the area. Each will provide a mix of residential and office space, along with pedestrian amenities in the form of waterfront esplanades and malls. Battery Park City's decked plazas, built over land claimed from the Hudson River, will be, except for emergency-vehicle use, a pedestrian haven. Manhattan Landing's planned amenities include a

Walkways link the new Toronto City Hall with older government buildings to the right, creating a civic-center pedestrian district.

hotel, marina, sports facility, department store and oceanographic center.

Both are within easy walking distance of the city's financial, world-trade and insurance districts, and government offices. A walk to work is a tonic in most seasons, especially for the sedentary worker, who makes up such a large proportion of the urban work force.

The amenities of pedestrian districts like Battery Park City and Manhattan Landing will attract and enchant residents, office workers and visitors to lower Manhattan. Day- and night-time activity will support restaurants and shops which cannot survive in a single-use district operating only during office hours.

Civic Centers as Pedestrian Districts

Man's sense of powerlessness in today's

large, complex urban setting, the need to restore a sense of community in an age of onrushing technology—these are by now familiar themes. By eroding the streets's age-old function as meeting place and forum, thus making the street uninviting, a place to be shunned, the automobile has played a role in the loss of community identification.

In an attempt to make cities less impersonal places and city government more responsive to its citizens and manageable by its officials, efforts are under way in many places to create local units of government centered on identifiable communities within each city.

Planners have suggested a variety of population sizes for an urban module which could serve as a manageable unit of design and administration, and retain community identification at the same time. Ebenezer Howard, a court reporter in England for whom planning was an avocation and nineteenth-century London a thoroughly disagreeable place, thought 30,000 would be the right population for such an urban unit. His disciple, Lewis Mumford, points out that this is the very size Leonardo da Vinci selected when he proposed to the Duke of Milan to relieve the congestion and foul disorders of sixteenth-century Milan by designing ten cities of 30,000 population each.

London's thirty-two boroughs have an average population of 230,000 each. In New York City, 130,000 is the approximate population of each of its sixty-two planning districts. Whatever the body's size, its heart should be a community civic center.

The building directory of each center might read something like this:

Officials: Community Offices of Congressman, State Senator, State Assemblyman, City Councilman, School Board, Planning Board; local service heads of Police, Fire, Health, Social Services.

A plaza can take many forms. This open space at Jacob Riis Houses has been made into an amphitheater for tenant and neighborhood use. The amphitheater is modeled on the Shakespearean theater at Stratford-on-Avon, England, and is designed both for a children's play area and for theatrical performances. (Pomerance & Breines, Architects; M. Paul Friedberg & Associates, Landscape Architects)

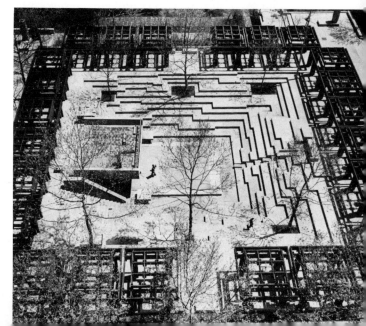

In this corner of the Boston Government Center, a sidewalk café recaptures pre-automobile pleasures; the lighting and paving are pedestrian-oriented; and the effort (seen to the right) to preserve older buildings of architectural quality succeeds.

Services: Local processing of rent, consumer and municipal service complaints; issuance of licenses.

Facilities: Community auditorium, exhibition hall, library and meeting rooms.

The community civic center would advance public convenience and government visibility. It would be a listening post to receive the comments and suggestions of the people in whose behalf the services are undertaken. The centers would serve as meeting places where city-wide and local officials could discuss common concerns with community members and seek to formulate common responses.

Each center might be planned around a vehicle-free public open space. This process could take place over a period of years as existing public buildings, which generally relate to no scheme whatsoever, are abandoned and new structures, forming the components of the community civic center, are completed. The sharing of facilities by government agencies would be less costly and more efficient in the long run than the present disorganized rental practices.

The open space might take the form of a square. Cities that developed before the machine age invariably had squares for the watering of horses and selling of wares. Here public meetings were held and gossip exchanged. The square has not fared well in the modern city.* Gordon Cullen, the British planner, writes in his book *Townscape:*

The idea of the town as a place of assembly, of social intercourse, of meeting, was taken for granted throughout the whole of human civilization up to the twentieth century. You might assemble in the Forum at Pompeii or round the market cross, but you still assembled; it was a ritual proper to man, both a rite

* Due to the lack of squares in New York City, many events suitable for presentation in a public square are now held in parks. The result has been substantial damage to park land, since parks were not designed for such intensive use.

Present view (left) of the City Hall area in New York. Its park setting is reduced to a parking lot. The New York Civic Center (right) as it might have been. This view looking north shows a pedestrian mall extending from City Hall to a new Municipal Building. The traffic-free mall is flanked to the left by a proposed Executive Office Building and to the right by the existing Municipal Building. (Max Abramovitz, Simon Breines and Robert W. Cutler, Architects)

and a right. Nor in the general way did you have to explain whether your motives were proper or profane. Men are gregarious and expect to meet. In all ages but ours, that is.[7]

The pedestrian district comprising the community civic center and public square would provide each community with a focus. Residents, after arrival by subway or bus, would find all the government agencies serving their community within easy walking distance. Local officials, just down the hall from one another, or a short distance across the square, would benefit from improved communication and coordination of activities. The regular flow of people arriving at the center to use city services, or for community meetings, free of the disruptive effect of the automobile, would have the opportunity to mingle and chat in a relaxed community setting.

Cultural events could take place in the center auditorium and exhibition hall, or outdoors in the public square. These facilities would encourage additional cultural activity, drawing on both city-wide resources and home-grown talent. New

In Rio de Janeiro the cheerful, decorative sidewalks reveal genuine concern for pedestrian amenities. The art of paving flourishes in such an atmosphere.

York City museums might display exhibits at various community civic centers, thus enriching the lives of many more residents than they now reach.*

With each community having its own civic-local-government-cultural center, planned around a vehicle-free public square, a high degree of local allegiance and identification will be achieved.[8]

The necessary larger allegiance, to the entire city, can be symbolized by a city-wide civic center which is also a pedestrian district. Some cities—Philadelphia and

* The Whitney Museum of American Art on Manhattan's Upper East Side has moved in the direction of reaching out to residents of other communities by opening a branch in the city's financial district.

Street clock, Nicollet Mall.

Toronto, for example—have created such districts. In Boston the Government Center, comprising City Hall, federal buildings, hotels, office towers, shops and functioning landmarks, forms a large, vehicle-free public square.

A visitor to New York's City Hall area, by comparison, finds vehicular chaos. City Hall itself is an architectural gem and national landmark. It is on a slight rise which commands a magnificent view of the Brooklyn Bridge, a bridge which glorifies walking, and again has become a popular

footway across the East River from Manhattan to Brooklyn. The plaza in front of City Hall, however, serves as a parking lot for official cars. From time to time efforts are made to ban the parking, but then are rejected on grounds of political practicality, since it is a status symbol of sorts to have a City Hall parking sticker.

Few New Yorkers, including city officials, are aware of the spot in City Hall Plaza where the Declaration of Independence was read and published to the American Army on July 9, 1776, in the presence of General Washington, five days after its adoption by the Continental Congress. The plaque honoring the event is blocked by motor vehicles and comes into view only after the official cars depart.

Major traffic arteries cut City Hall off from nearby municipal, state and federal buildings. Although three rapid-transit lines serve the area, the tens of thousands of government employees arriving each day must combat traffic-congested streets to reach their offices.

In 1962 the New York City Board of Estimate approved plans developed by a team of architects for a New York Civic Center. The key elements of the proposed ABC Plan are:

connection of the government buildings by a traffic-free pedestrian area;

a ceremonial landscaped mall, lined with trees, benches and sculpture;

an underground arcade system with shops and restaurants, giving access to building and transit lines at subway level;

a pedestrian connection to the Brooklyn Bridge walkway; and

a municipal garage below the arcades, of sufficient capacity to clear the civic center area of street parking.

Though formally authorized, the city never carried out the plan, on grounds that a tunnel was needed to carry vehicular traffic under the civic center, rather than the street-level diversion of cars proposed by the architects. The latter method, city

Urban art is being relentlessly destroyed by vehicular vibrations and pollution. This pre-Columbian sculpture was lent by the Mexican government and put on display in the Seagram Plaza on Park Avenue. The automobile might have claimed the magnificent head as victim had it remained here for long. In pedestrian districts, urban art will find a compatible environment.

officials feared, would saturate the area with cars. The tunnel proved utterly impractical because of the enormous cost and the presence of subway lines, but it took years of palaver to reach this conclusion. Meanwhile, costs rose and some city agencies, like the Police Department, lost patience and built on sites outside the civic center area. Had the technique of pedestrian engineering been available, the fifteen acres of the proposed civic center could have been experimentally closed to traffic by the use of wooden police bar-

Outdoor sculpture in Riis Houses Plaza in New York City. Climbable and vandal-proof. (William Tarr, sculptor)

riers, a planning device involving a minimum outlay of funds and effort.

A New York civic center pedestrian district is as valid today as when first proposed. Municipal business and the public are served by linking government buildings for convenient access. Office workers and residents of lower Manhattan could enjoy its amenities by day, and in place of the present after-dark deathlike stillness, residents, strollers and tourists would be attracted at night by its urban vitality. Chinatown and the South Street Seaport Maritime Museum are within easy walking distance. A mini-bus system could link the civic center with Wall Street, Battery Park City, Manhattan Landing and the Battery Park promenade overlooking New York City harbor.

Urban Strollways

Widened sidewalks, park streets, downtown islands, thru-block walkways and other pedestrian areas provide their own justification. But when several of them can be linked together in a continuous chain of traffic-free walking situations, the result becomes a triumph of pedestrian engineering. We then have what we call an urban strollway system. The whole has become greater than the sum of its parts.

A Manhattan urban strollway system might connect several key city points: the United Nations, Park Avenue, Rockefeller

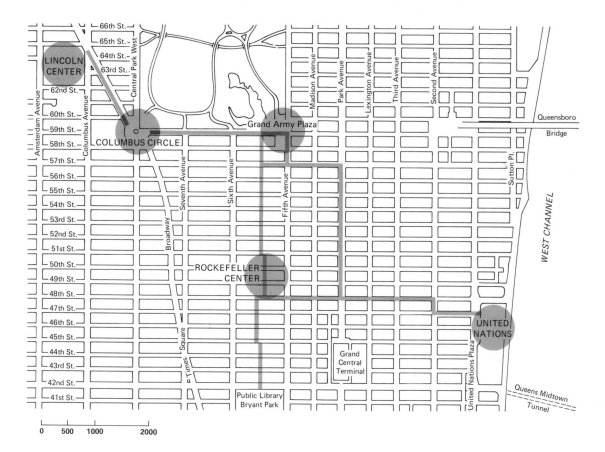

This proposed urban strollway system links up with key points in Manhattan. (Pomerance & Breines, Architects)

Center, Bryant and Central parks, Columbus Circle and Lincoln Center. Unlike a vehicular street, which must be completely realized along its entire length to be usable, a strollway can grow link by link, and each strollway link is usable from the start.

The pedestrian is sensitive to one of the most important factors in his environment—the surface under foot. A city con-

cerned with its pedestrians will be aware of the surfaces on which they walk. Walking surfaces need not always be concrete and asphalt. Certain pavings are more congenial for walking than others. Slightly rough textures satisfy because they offer the shoe a secure grip. Examples are bricks, cobblestones, flagstones, asphalt paving blocks and boardwalks. People who have known the pleasures of seaside

A thru-block walkway in Stockholm.

boardwalks would welcome this delightful effect on urban strollways. We are not necessarily suggesting wooden strolling surfaces in pedestrian districts, but rather that the qualities of resiliency associated with boardwalks be captured for everyday city use.

The strollway's identifying mark will be the special color and texture of its paving. The paving design will be decorative and functional. An example of this technique is the Freedom Trail in Boston, a continuous strip of red bricks inlaid in the sidewalk, serving as a visual guide to the Revolutionary landmarks of the city. The design of paving patterns will indicate lanes for walking, cycling and mini-vehicles. Sitting and quiet areas will be delineated by planting and benches; but also by areas of cobbled blocks and bricks designed to discourage mini-vehicle use.

Street signs and street furniture can be designed for the slower pace of pedestrians and mini-vehicles. Street signs will be less blatant when no need exists to see them from a passing bus or taxi, and lighting can be less strident where open spaces no longer serve as highways. Along with humans, trees and plants will thrive on a strollway.

Office workers, shoppers and strollers can use the traffic-free streets and open spaces of an urban strollway to reach a variety of destinations. Outdoor cafés will flourish in a setting free of the noise and pollution of cars, trucks and buses. Cafés need not be crowded on narrow sidewalks, but will be arranged for the functional needs of eating, people-watching and conversation.

The steady flow of pedestrians, day and night, will encourage restaurants and shops to advertise their location on the strollway. Once an urban strollway is established, new buildings and existing ones will orient themselves to it in terms of entrance lobbies and plazas. Articulation with subways and underground streets are logical developments.

Our emphasis on walking and pedestrians may create the impression that an urban strollway is only for the young and vigorous. Actually, the old and infirm, those least agile at dodging vehicles or loping across wide, vehicle-clogged avenues within the thirty-five-second period of grace allotted them by traffic lights, would be among the main beneficiaries of pedestrianism. Paving opportunities in pedestrian districts can, for example, guide the blind by a walkway Braille system. At present, the blind have an agonizing time crossing city streets.

A strollway which attracts numerous pedestrians at all hours will afford the elderly—in fact, all city dwellers—with more security than exists on most urban streets today. A well-used city street is apt to be a safe street. The safety of the street works best, Jane Jacobs points out, where people use and enjoy them, without being aware that their very presence is helping to police them.

Skeptics of pedestrianism contend that something of value is lost when foot and wheel are separated. Urbanity, goes the

The Hamilton Mall in Allentown, Pennsylvania, is a contemporary example of a covered shopping street. The canopies are constructed of Plexiglas acrylic plastic.

argument, requires both pedestrians and vehicles to produce the contrast of tempo and color, of purpose and shape that is the very throb of city life.[9]

In actual fact, conventional vehicles discourage street life; walking stimulates it. Abundant pedestrian activity and the presence of mini-vehicles, a safe and non-polluting form of transport, will animate the open spaces of a city. Urbanity will thrive in pedestrian areas!

CHAPTER V
THE BICYCLE AS URBAN TRANSPORT

The mini-vehicle need not be invented. It already exists in numerous forms. The bicycle is one of the most important.

The bicycle may seem old-fashioned, but then, man himself is a pretty old-fashioned machine, bubbling with unexploited, nonpolluting energy. Suggestions of vehicles having two or more wheels and propelled by the muscular effort of the rider are to be found in very early times; they appear on ancient Egyptian and Babylonian bas-reliefs. Pompeian frescoes depict winged figures riding sticks supported by two wheels.[1] A stained-glass window in the parish church at Stoke Poges, Buckinghamshire, England, dated 1642, shows a cherub astride a wheeled form of hobby-horse blowing a trumpet. It was not until the nineteenth century,

Widespread bicycle use in the nineteenth century influenced fashions.

240.

(a) 'Ladies' cycling dress' 'The coat gracefully defines the figure . . . the knickers and leggings complete the dress.' (1895.) (b) Cycling costume 'adapted for cycling, ample ease being provided where most required'. (1890.)

THE PEDESTRIAN REVOLUTION

TRACING FROM A STAINED-GLASS WINDOW
IN AN OLD ENGLISH CHURCH: DATE, 1642.

however, that mere mortals took up the bicycle.

Cycling soon became a world-wide phenomenon. By 1890, over three hundred bicycle factories were operating day and night in the United States, filling orders from all parts of the country. In far-off Moscow, Tolstoy pedaled silently and happily about on an English-made machine, while in New York City a police Bicycle Squad was organized "for the better protection of pedestrians against careless bicycle riders."[2] By the end of the nineteenth century, four million Americans owned bicycles.

Glen Olds (for whom the Oldsmobile is named), Henry Ford and the Chevrolet and Duesenberg brothers were among the automotive pioneers who cut their inventive eyeteeth as bicycle builders.

The bicycle was the first machine to be mass-produced for personal transportation. Bicycle technology paved the way for the car. Pneumatic and cord tires, ball bearings, differential steering, seamless steel tubing and expansion brakes—all were developed for the bicycle. The first automobiles ran on roads upgraded from cow paths for bicycle use.

With the auto's spreading popularity, the nation's ardor for the bicycle waned. In America, the bicycle joined the horse as an extinct means of transport. It became a child's toy. For large numbers of the world's population, however, the bicycle has continued to play a major transportation role. We have only to think of China and India, having between them almost one third of the world's population, where bicycle use is widespread. Or of tiny North Vietnam, where the bicycle has played an important transport role in over a quarter century of fighting with two of the most technically advanced nations in the world—France and the United States. Or of Amsterdam, where during the rush hour 60 percent of all journeys to and from the central area of the city are made by bicycle, and only 10 percent by car.[3]

But the past decade has wrought revolutionary changes in the United States.

STREETS WITHOUT CARS

Bicycles have become a billion-dollar business. The year 1972 marked the first time since the appearance of the Model T Ford that Americans purchased more bikes—over twelve million—than cars. As a transportation landmark, 1972 may match 1913, the first year more automobiles were produced than wagons and buggies.

The bicycle's renewed appeal is based in part on environmental and health considerations. It needs no fuel, gives off no fumes, and makes almost no noise. "Bicycles," the distinguished heart specialist Dr. Paul Dudley White once said, "are the answer for both brain and body." Improved circulation, good muscle tone, weight control and relaxed spirits are some of the beneficial side effects of bike use. These help to reduce the fatigue of daily work. Increasingly, doctors prescribe this medicine: one bicycle, to be used daily.

More time for leisure has helped to boost the bicycle's popularity. For some,

Bikeway in Holland, safely separated from traffic. Surely no one would claim that these contented, serene Dutch cyclists are deprived in any manner because they are pedaling their way instead of riding in an automobile.

Chinese street scene.

it is an outlet against the mechanization of work and daily life. For still others, bicycling has even greater significance: it is a voyage of self-discovery. The American author William Saroyan writes: "I was not yet sixteen when I understood a great deal, from having ridden bicycles for so long, about style, speed, grace, purpose, value, form, integrity, health, humor, music, breathing, and finally and perhaps best of all the relationship between the beginning and the end."[4]

These millions of bikes demand to be used. But in the larger, built-up cities, the automobile simply leaves no room for the bicycle.

City parks have been the only exception. In 1966 Mayor Lindsay closed Central Park to cars at certain times on an experimental basis. The results were dramatic. Bike riders thronged the park's six miles of roadway running through the center of Manhattan Island. The air-pollution count in the park fell. Manhattan auto traffic was able to find other routes without difficulty on weekends and on the summer evenings during the week when the park was closed. Soon the experimental weekend-closing became permanent and was extended to Prospect Park in Brooklyn. Mayor Lindsay's bold action proved to be the most popular one of his eight-year administration: an excellent example of the acceptability of mini-vehicles if proper conditions for their use are created.

But recreational cycling in parks is not the same as safe and convenient conditions for traveling to work and school, or for shopping. In the streets, bicyclists must compete with cars, trucks, buses and taxis. It is an unequal contest.

Those who cycle on traffic-filled streets do so at great peril. Here a London bicyclist prepares to do battle:

I'm leaving behind me the safety and security of the park [Hyde Park], and any minute now I shall be flinging myself into the chaos of London's worst traffic junction. All those motorists are wrapped in tin and armour-plate, but there's only the naked me to set against them and their 50–100 horsepower. Still, here goes. . .[5]

A popular American bicycle handbook offers this sobering advice:

[When riding,] look for openings in traffic, driveways, streets, garages, etc., that you can duck into should the need arise. Try to plan where you would go should you and the bike part company. The natural tendency in a collision situation is to try desperately to stop. Many times your interests will be better served by launching yourself over an obstacle. Far better to hit the pavement at an angle than a car head-on.[6]

Little wonder the United States Consumer Product Safety Commission has concluded that the bicycle is the most dangerous single product in the American home. The critical bicycle safety problem is the incompatibility between cyclists and the automobile.

But death and injury are not the only dangers. Traffic streets are cloaked in pollutants. Bicyclists are at nose level with a lethal mix, breathing it in faster and harder than drivers or pedestrians.

In short, without the physical separation of bicycles from vehicular traffic, the bicycle will never be able to fulfill its potential role as a means of urban transport. Yet in most cities a separate bikeway system, using other than existing street space, would cost many millions of dollars. If construction of a separate bikeway will cost too much, is there any prospect for the bicycle as a partial transportation alternative to the automobile?

THE PEDESTRIAN REVOLUTION

The answer is a resounding yes—through the creation of what we term an *urban bikeway*. An urban bikeway system would be created by reserving some existing roadbeds for exclusive cycle use. Motor vehicles would operate on other streets. Pedestrians would continue to use the sidewalks of an urban bikeway, though without being victimized by fumes and noise.

To be safe, a bikeway must be free of conventional vehicles. To be convenient, it must connect the main residential areas with the central business district. These basic concepts can be applied in different ways in different cities. What follows is an example of a possible Manhattan network of bikeway streets.

In Manhattan, a bikeway would naturally begin with Central Park, which stretches down the middle of the island from 110th to 59th streets. The temporary closing of Central Park to automobiles, a proven success, would thus be made permanent. By riding, or even walking their bikes to the park, bicyclists will find safe and convenient routes exiting at Central Park South and Seventh Avenue, as shown on the Manhattan urban bikeway map. The suggested route would follow Seventh Avenue to Times Square, and then down Broadway to 23rd Street and Fifth Avenue. It would continue down Fifth Avenue to Washington Square, and then along Thompson Street, and easterly on Broome Street to Broadway. From there it would continue on Broadway to Battery Park, at the southern tip of Manhattan Island.

Seventh Avenue is the first bikeway link south of Central Park. It begins at 59th Street and runs one-way south. Broadway also runs one-way south from 59th Street. It can absorb much of the vehicular traffic now operating on Seventh Avenue between Central Park South and Times Square.

Broadway follows a diagonal course down Manhattan. At key points where Broadway intersects the gridiron system, of which it is not a part, it introduces an

None but the brave, or foolhardy, rides bicycles on city streets. The bicycle and the motor vehicle are incompatible; urban bikeways will separate them.

extra traffic flow which the gridiron is not equipped to handle. This is why Broadway has always caused major traffic complications both at Times Square and Herald Square. By removing vehicular traffic from Broadway below Times Square, congestion at these intersections would be greatly relieved.

At 23rd Street, Broadway cuts across Fifth Avenue. At this point, Fifth Avenue seems a more logical link in the bikeway system. Traffic along this stretch of Fifth Avenue is relatively light because the avenue dead-ends at Washington Square Park.

Thompson Street is a continuation of Fifth Avenue south of Washington Square Park. Since Thompson Street dead-ends at Canal Street, Broome Street is suggested to bring the bikeway east to Broadway. The bikeway then continues south on Broadway to Battery Park, overlooking New York City's harbor.

Traffic lights along the urban bikeway would control the east-west movement of conventional vehicles, as well as the north-south movement on the bikeway of bicycles and pedestrians.

Except for emergency vehicles, all conventional motor vehicles would be excluded from the urban bikeway. The two-hundred-foot north-south block, so common in Manhattan, lessens the difficulty of servicing buildings and shops on

Bicycle booby trap. It is not only the moving vehicle which is a hazard, for the door swung open suddenly from a parked car can demolish the urban cyclist just as effectively.

the bikeway. This is because building entrances are never more than one hundred feet from an east-west crosstown street, where conventional vehicles would continue to operate.

As more people shift from autos to bikes, there will be some relief from motor vehicle traffic. Forty-three percent of all urban work trips made by car in the United States are four miles or less, and in nine out of ten of these trips, the driver is the sole occupant. Bicycles are the fastest form of urban transport for trips up to three miles. A perfect match of vehicle with need.

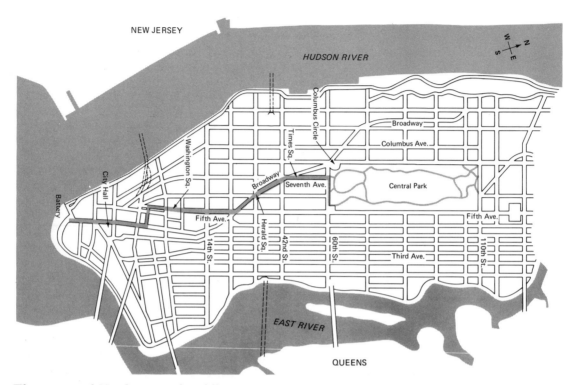

The proposed Manhattan urban bikeway system would run down the middle of the island from Central Park to the Battery. The bikeway could begin modestly enough—as a single lane physically separated from vehicles on a traffic street—and could develop, through experimentation and by stages, into an urban bikeway system involving whole streets. (Pomerance & Breines, Architects)

In addition, current bicycle-travel volumes do not reflect the number of people who would like to use bicycles, but rather the lack of safe facilities for bike travel. Urban bikeways are like highways: a good system will generate increased use.

Two-way movement of bicycles and tricycles, together with other mini-vehicles, would be permitted on the bikeway roadbed.

The bikeway, with its slow-moving nonpolluting vehicles, is compatible with pedestrian use. Benches would be available for sitting. The sidewalks of the bikeway might be widened to accommodate double rows of trees, or trees could be planted in the center of the roadbed, both to enhance the street scene and to separate the passage of mini-vehicles traveling north and south. The two functions of the urban bikeway—pedal and pedestrian—would rejuvenate street life. Walkers and cyclists are natural window-shoppers

Urban bikeway scene.

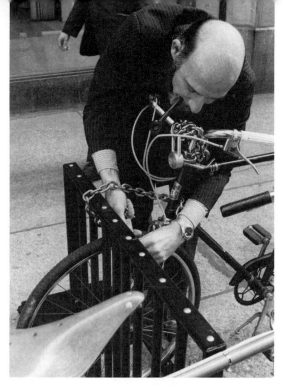

With the aid of locks and chains, this bicyclist hopes to prevent the theft of his bike. A more cautious cyclist would also detach the front wheel and carry it away. Theft inhibits urban bike use. The bicycle rental service eliminates this problem.

and restaurant customers. Crowds make for security and festivity. The bikeway-strollway would be a cyclist-pedestrian paradise!

A bikeway free of automobile traffic is essential to the greater use of bicycles in cities, but a bikeway system by itself cannot solve all the problems facing urban cyclists. They still have to find ways to store their bikes in tall apartment houses and office buildings, and they have to wage a daily, losing struggle with petty thieves and vandals. It is not an uncommon sight in theft-conscious New York City to come upon a bicycle owner who keeps his bike in his apartment for safe-keeping, or

brings it up to the office. In San Francisco, the Bicycle Coalition warns it members:

Never leave your bike unprotected. Unfortunately, the minimum adequate protection is a heavy-duty, case-hardened chain and lock; but most people can wear them comfortably around the waist.

Under these conditions, bike ownership is risky and expensive. What is needed is a rental service, much like the present car-rental systems.

Suppose it were possible to pick up a rental bike at convenient depots in residential areas, ride it to work and leave it at another depot near the office. As proposed by Pomerance & Breines, the rental service could be based on about four hundred depots scattered conveniently in Manhattan's residential and business districts. Each depot would be staffed by an attendant who distributes and receives the bikes and also keeps them in working condition. The bike storage depots may be located in any of hundreds of garages now in use in Manhattan, or they may be in small stores or on the street floor of buildings.

The rental service may be more readily understood if a subscriber is followed through a typical day of bike use in Manhattan.

Let us assume that Daisy Jones lives on West 78th Street near Broadway and

works on East 32nd Street and Third Avenue, a distance of about two and a half miles. As a subscriber, Daisy has a card, color-coded differently each month, which she presents at a nearby depot at 76th Street and Columbus Avenue. When Daisy gives up her card, she gets a bike which is a simple machine of a single, distinctive design, with a package carrier. She may, of course, ride this rented bike anywhere, but we shall assume that she prefers to use the safe urban bikeway we have already described, to get to her job.

The most direct way for Daisy is to pick up the bikeway in Central Park, one block away from the Columbus Avenue bike depot. She would then follow the bikeway route downtown to 30th Street and Broadway. Here she would exit, and follow 30th Street, an eastbound side street, to Third

A modest example of pedestrian engineering. People arriving in a pedestrian district by subway can complete their journey on foot or by mini-vehicle.

Avenue, where another depot would be located. Only at the beginning and end of her ride to work, when she is not on the bikeway, does Daisy share the street with conventional vehicles. But traffic is not as heavy, and moves at far less dangerous speeds on east-west side streets than on north-south avenues. For the major part of her ride, Daisy enjoys the safety of the bikeway. At the 30th Street-Third Avenue depot Daisy would receive a color-coded card in return for the bike. From here she has only two blocks to walk to her office.

At the end of the day, Daisy can obtain a bike from the depot by turning in the card. If, during the day, she wants to buy theater tickets at Times Square, she could pick up a bike at any depot and leave it at the Times Square depot. At all times, she either has a bike or rental card.

Bike-rental subscriptions could be issued on a monthly basis, like railroad commutation tickets. During each period of use, the card may be exchanged for a bike as many times as desired, and the bike can be kept for as long as needed. Thus, Daisy's subscription card would also provide her with a bicycle for recreation over weekends and on holidays. She never has to be concerned about storage, and she will always have a bicycle in good running condition whenever she wants one.

The bike-rental service could operate as a private business under a municipal fran-

Mini-vehicles will shuttle bicycles back and forth among depots as needed.

chise. The annual rental per cycle might be $150. This comes to about forty cents per day. In Manhattan alone, the number of subscribers might reach 90,000.[7]

What about the subscriber who pays the month's rental of $12.50 and then keeps the bicycle? The bicycle will cost only about $25. It will also be of a unique, recognizable design so that it cannot easily be sold. The important point, however, is that one can steal the bicycle but not the service. Unless the user keeps turning the bicycle in at depots, he is simply not getting the benefits of storage and maintenance which go with the rental.

What happens if the weather is clear in the morning when subscribers ride their bikes to work, but turns to rain or snow in the evening, causing many to go home by subway or bus? To handle this, as well as the imbalance caused by those who end up their day's bike use at different depots, the rental service will have several bike carriers shuttling the machines back and forth between depots as required.

What about bike use in winter? In Sweden, which has far more severe weather than most cities in the United States, the response to this is: "There is no bad weather for bikes, only bad clothing." Bicycle use in Stockholm continues year-round, even on those days when radio and television warn automobile drivers to stay away from the city because of snow conditions. As with conventional streets, snow will be cleared from the urban bikeway. Those cyclists who prefer not to ride in rain or snow can use the other transportation facilities now available to them.

The most difficult question is political. What is the likelihood of government officials approving an urban bikeway? At first blush, the candid response must be, "Not good."

Take New York City, for example. Mayor Lindsay sensed the political capital latent in the bicycle movement and opened Central Park to bikes. But when it came to viewing the bicycle beyond its recreational role, as an important transportation

Members of the League of American Wheelmen on review in Boston. The League had political clout, something present-day cyclists sorely need.

mode for moving large numbers of people to work and school, he faltered.

Two "Bike to Work Days" tell the story. On the first such day, in 1971, Mayor Lindsay, still euphoric over the success of his Central Park experiment, joined one thousand cyclists for a part of the five-mile ride from Fifth Avenue and 60th Street, downtown to his office at City Hall. The event sought to dramatize the bicycle's potential as a vehicle for commuting between home and work. A year later, after proposals to create a commuter lane reserved for bicyclists on Fifth Avenue incurred the stiff opposition of merchants, the bicyclists repeated the trip, but this time without the mayor.

The bicyclists had become a political embarrassment to the mayor. Not well organized or influential, the bike lobby was no match for the merchants. The token efforts undertaken by New York City officials clearly reflect the bike lobby's political weakness. These efforts include two hundred lamppost signs reading, "BICYCLE ROUTE," to alert auto drivers to the presence of bicyclists on the street, but affording cyclists no protection; some bicycle racks near public buildings; and a booklet on bicycle safety. Concerning the last item, one angry cyclist commented, "We need safe bike lanes, not a booklet on safety!"

But the time for change is ripe. In 1973, 15.3 million bicycles were sold in this country. Adults now account for 65 percent of the market. Seventy million bicycles are in use. (This compares with 100 million passenger cars.) Bicyclists have become too large a group to ignore. Congress recognizes this. In 1973 the Federal Highway Act provided funds for bikeways for the first time. A Bicycle Institute of America survey shows that almost every state legislature has major bicycle proposals under consideration. California, the most populous of the states, is already applying a portion of both its highway gas tax and local sales tax for bikeways.

Like any other group in this country which wants action on its behalf, bike riders will need to organize and make themselves heard. Bicyclists did precisely this nearly a century ago, when they organized the League of American Wheelmen. A national organization with a membership of 100,000, the league was one of the most powerful citizen groups in the United States. It fought and won battles for bikeways to replace rutted horse-and-

States *Scientific American:* "Man on a bicycle ranks first in efficiency among traveling animals and machines in terms of energy consumed in moving a certain distance as a function of body weight. The rate of energy consumption for a bicyclist (about .15 calorie per gram per kilometer) is approximately a fifth of that for an unaided walking man (about .75 calorie per gram per kilometer)."

buggy roads. The latter were the bane of cyclists, causing them to be pitched over the handlebars into the mud, often landing headfirst (whence the term "header").

Once bicyclists are well organized, political leaders will pay attention to their needs. Then, and only then, will the bicycle, a vehicle of superb craftsmanship whose use benefits the environment while providing healthy exercise, come into its own as a significant means of urban transportation.

CHAPTER VI
OTHER MINI-VEHICLES

Like the bicycle, the other mini-vehicles we propose are noiseless, nonpolluting and maneuverable, to suit the winding ways of pedestrians. They are faster than walking, but slower than conventional vehicles. They are intended to mingle with, not mangle, the pedestrian—to "rub shoulders" with pedestrians without fatal consequences. After the Crimean War, Florence Nightingale set down the precept "The hospital shall not harm the patient." In pedestrian districts, the mini-vehicle shall not harm the pedestrian.

Many of us already use mini-vehicles. The supermarket is an example. Upon entering the supermarket, a pedestrian area, we select shopping carts, a form of mini-vehicle. Supermarket customers do not realize they are providing the energy to

Electric-powered tractor-trains carrying passengers along Fifth Avenue in New York City. Tractor-trains will be enclosed for passenger comfort during poor weather, will have roll-back roofs for use on good days.

This foot-powered vehicle is inappropriate for mingling with conventional vehicles, but would be in its element in a pedestrian district.

make the merchandizing machinery work, partly because the shopping cart assumes much of the burden. From the entrance door to the check-out lane, the supermarket is an example of the mini-vehicle facilitating the daily activity of pedestrians.

Of the large variety of mini-vehicles, the tractor-train is the most important. Powered by an electric tractor unit pulling a line of tractor-cars, it is the workhorse of the pedestrian district. Open-air passenger-carrying tractor-trains now operate in Disneyland and on fairgrounds. Pedestrian-district tractor-trains, used year-round, will be enclosed for passenger comfort during wet or cold weather, with roll-back roofs for use on warm, sunny days. They will cruise through the district on regular schedules, with major pick-up and drop-off points close to garages and bus stops at its periphery, and near subway stations within the district.

Among the users of the tractor-train will be the elderly, disabled and handicapped. And let's be frank, some perfectly healthy people don't like to walk, even under the best conditions. Max Beerbohm, the English satirist, is an amusing and articulate spokesman for this group. Walking, Beerbohm was convinced, stops the brain. With considerable relish, he boasted, "It is a fact that not once in all my life have I gone out for a walk." More power to Beerbohm and his latter-day sedentary followers! The tractor-train is the answer for people who can't, or won't, walk in a pedestrian district.

There will also be tractor-train cars designed to transport goods to the buildings and shops in the district, and service cars to convey mail and telephone equipment, for example. The design of these cars will relate to building entrances and freight elevators, making it possible to uncouple units and move them directly into buildings for off-street unloading. (This process is discussed in greater detail in the next chapter.)

Electric-powered vehicles, considered futuristic by some, have roots in early automotive history. In 1900, most cars in America were electric. Even Henry Ford's wife drove one—a 1914 Detroit Electric. But compared to the gasoline-powered car, the electric vehicle was expensive and

Tricycles are well suited for adult use as transport and as package carriers. They are simple and safe to operate. Note the passenger tractor-train in the background.

slow. In addition, a gas-driven vehicle's range was greater, while an electric car required a time-consuming battery recharge every sixty miles.

In pedestrian districts, electric vehicles would be in their natural element. Slow speeds, not exceeding fifteen miles an hour, are desirable, and limits on operational distance pose no serious problem. Changing the battery now takes no longer than gassing up. The battery is recharged by being plugged into any electrical outlet.

Electric-powered mini-buses, seating ten to fifteen passengers each, can be used during off-peak passenger periods, when tractor units are deployed to haul goods

and equipment, and in pedestrian district areas where limited passenger travel does not justify the use of a tractor-train.

Two-seat, self-driven mini-cars are another form of mini-vehicle. They are now in use on Amsterdam streets. Called "witcar," or white car, these golf-cart sized, high-domed electric vehicles can be rented

Bikes, trikes and pedestrians enjoy sharing the Atlantic City Boardwalk, with its resilient wood surface.

Three-wheeled, battery-powered scooters could be made available in pedestrian districts on a nominal rental basis, or as a free service.

by Amsterdamers who join a witcar co-operative union. As explained in the *New York Times,* a member of the cooperative takes a car from one of the witcar stations and pays the equivalent of three and a half cents a minute until he checks it in at another station in the city. At the second station the car is recharged in six minutes and

ready for the next driver. Each member gets his own coded key, which is used to turn on one meter at the departure station and shut off another at the arrival station. A computer calculates the charge and registers it automatically on the user's account. By 1975, if all goes well, the system will expand from five stations and thirty-five mini-cars to fifteen stations and over a hundred cars.

The witcar operates on conventional streets. In Amsterdam, where a high percentage of central-area rush-hour journeys are by bicycle, this may work. In most cities, however, conventional streets are a maelstrom of trucks, buses and cars. Like the pedestrians they serve, we do not believe that these slow, small-scale transports can operate safely under such conditions. But in traffic-free pedestrian districts, they are an ideal conveyance.

Tractor-trains and mini-buses would charge fares, or local government might subsidize part or all of the costs. People could hire mini-taxis, carrying two passengers each, and rent mini-cars, on a basis similar to the bike-rental service described

Roller skates are used in many industrial plants to expedite the handling of small parts. This simple means of transportation is appropriate in pedestrian districts. Skates can be carried in the subway or on buses, and then used to complete the journey. During lunchtime, or after work, people could skate for recreation.

An array of mini-vehicles.

in Chapter V, or to the Amsterdam coded-key system.

The automobile industry, justly chastised for its indifference to the adverse environmental impact of the car, and for failure to foresee the energy shortage, even contributing to it by the production of increasingly larger, energy-intensive models, is striving to catch up with events through an expensive change-over to smaller, less polluting models. There is increasing recognition that even compact cars have a limited role to play in urban centers. Henry Ford II writes: "What we need and are now beginning to see, in addition to cars and mass transit, are new kinds of vehicles and systems designed to carry people quickly, conveniently and efficiently where neither cars nor conventional transit can do the job as well."[1]

The auto industry would do well to turn its attention to mini-vehicles. In any event, the Pedestrian Revolution will not permit the massive congestion and pollution of our cities to continue. Since pedestrians cannot be made smaller, vehicles will have to shrink instead.

The bicycle is a self-propelled form of mini-vehicle; roller skates are also in this category. The traffic police chief of Rome has banned roller skates from the streets, declaring them to be "not a means of transport." This is a view we do not share. Industry now uses skates as a means of travel within large plants. Anyone who has had some childhood experience in American cities knows the value of roller skates. The development of the ball-bearing wheel revolutionized roller-skating, making possible fast and exhilarating travel on city streets. But then came the usurpation of the street by the automobile. Today, skating is perilous for both children and adults. In a pedestrian district, or on an urban bikeway, it will be possible to skate to work or school. Roller-skate designers, sensing the renewal of interest in this means of transportation, are replacing the old-fashioned clunky skates that clasp on shoes with snappy multicolored sandal-skates in high-gloss plastic.

The more widespread use of bikes, trikes, skates and self-propelled scooters (used now with success by passengers and airline employees at Copenhagen's Kastrup Airport), to say nothing of walking, should add immeasurably to the physical and mental health of city dwellers. The human body has a natural ability to move efficiently and joyously. People-powered mini-vehicles are more than just a means of transportation; they are also fun, and under traffic-free conditions, they will be safe.

Mini-buses, for use in pedestrian districts or in the suburbs.

CHAPTER VII
THE FULLY DEVELOPED PEDESTRIAN DISTRICT

By experimentation and through experience, we will be able to learn the best ways to design and operate pedestrian districts. But pedestrian engineering need not start from scratch. Many examples of pedestrianism are already under way in cities throughout the world, as planners and architects respond to the ferment of the Pedestrian Revolution. Enough has been learned from the present and recalled from the past to permit us to sketch out a fully realized pedestrian district of the future.

An automobile driver will know he is arriving at a pedestrian district because traffic is routed around it. If he wants to enter, he must leave his car at one of the garages conveniently located on the edges of the district.

Times Square as a pedestrian district.

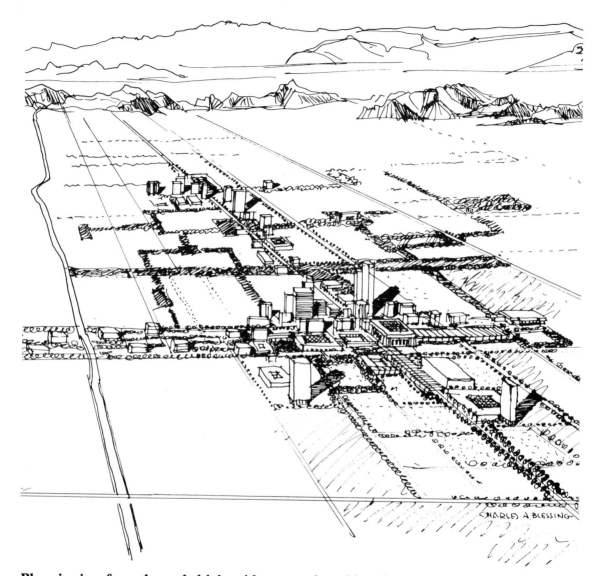

Phoenix rises from the asphalt! As with many other cities, the downtown district of Phoenix is dying. A major study undertaken for Phoenix by the American Institute of Architects proposes the pedestrianization of Central Avenue, the city's major avenue, and the development of a mass-transportation system. The sketch suggests how the gridiron street pattern of the downtown can be interwoven with major pedestrian areas, including residential districts. People living downtown will attract shops and restaurants. Mass transportation will permit the development of attractive, fume-free, tree-shaded downtown pedestrian areas which can compete more effectively with suburban shopping centers. (Sketch by Charles A. Blessing, Architect)

However, most people who work or live in a pedestrian district would use mass transportation. Those arriving by bus will alight at its periphery. In cities with subway systems, the district would include one or more stations. (A Times Square, midtown Manhattan or Wall Street pedestrian district would contain numerous stations.) Travelers arriving to the district by subway would enter office and residential buildings by way of shopping concourses at station level.

Whatever the means of arrival, a choice of mini-transport will be available to carry people to their destination. Travelers can ride a tractor-train, hail a mini-cab, or rent a bicycle or a mini-car. Or they can walk.

Circulation nodes will develop in pedestrian districts where tractor-trains pick up passengers and where bicycles and mini-cars may be rented. Arrival points at the edges of the district, where motorists leave their cars and passengers alight from buses and taxis, would be natural stations for the mini-vehicles operating within the pedestrian area. Subway stations are also logical mini-transport centers.

Trucks with equipment and supplies for delivery within the pedestrian district will discharge their loads at transfer depots at the outskirts of the district. These will not be conventional trucks, which, carrying the goods of a single company, wander through the streets half-full, hauling about

huge cubic volumes of empty, useless storage space.

Department stores long ago recognized the wisdom of pooling their delivery system into a single, separately operated United Parcel Service. This unification has paid off in concrete savings to the participant stores, because fewer men and vehicles are required to handle the same amount of goods.

Suppose we could expand the United Parcel Service concept to include the delivery of most goods and equipment. A given vehicle, or fleet of vehicles, could be assigned to carry all manner of shipments to a small destination area. Such vehicles would travel a shorter distance than existing trucks do, and would convey a far greater payload. This would help to rationalize distribution and cut down truck traffic outside pedestrian districts. (Pedestrian engineering, of course, is concerned also with reducing unnecessary vehicular movement outside areas specifically designated as pedestrian districts.)

The United Parcel Service is one already accepted service pattern that can be adapted to pedestrian districts; another is the post-office system. A post office performs two important functions: it provides a transfer point where mail from different areas can be sorted into bundles for buildings in a given section of the city, and it provides one carrier instead of many to

Pedestrians are people. In Seville, Spain (left), there is a recognition of this. Here *toldos*—awnings—protect shoppers from the hot sun. The street is old, the method archaic, but someone cares. In colder lands one finds enclosed shopping areas such as the Galleria in Milan, London's Burlington Arcade off Piccadilly, and the GUM Department Store on Red Square in Moscow. The IDS Center in Minneapolis (above), with its skylight roof, is a contemporary expression of a covered mall. (Philip Johnson and J. H. Burgee, Architects)

handle all the deliveries to be made to these buildings. If everyone in a city with mail for someone else made his own private delivery arrangements, massive confusion would ensue. Yet this is exactly what happens with the millions of tons of freight that are transported each day within a city. In a pedestrian district, the basic concept of "post-officing" would be applied to the delivery of goods.

United Parcel Service-type trucks would pull up for a curbless delivery at the loading platforms of the transfer depots located just outside the pedestrian district.

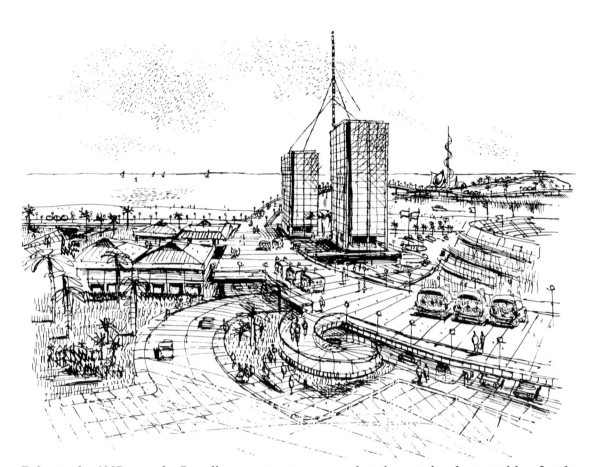

Prior to the 1967 war, the Israeli government sponsored an international competition for the redevelopment of Tel Aviv (left). To minimize disruption of the existing high-density business area, the plan shown here proposed to connect the business center with new sections of Tel Aviv and with the finger peninsula and island to be dredged from the sea by means of a system of raised boardwalks. These lightweight, economical arterial structures would be superimposed over the existing city fabric and reserved for pedestrians and mini-vehicles. A close look at this sketch shows how the boardwalks begin at the downtown center and run out to the new island park and to the beach-front hotel and residential district. Automobiles would continue to operate in the city as at present, independent of the boardwalk system. The proposal failed to win the competition, and subsequent hostilities in the Middle East led to the postponement of plans for Tel Aviv's redevelopment. (Pomerance & Breines, Architects; Albin Associates, Planners) A close-up view of the proposed Tel Aviv boardwalk system (above) shows electric-powered tractor-trains in operation and the relationship of the boardwalk to existing streets. Below the boardwalk, at street level, is space for parking and bus stations. (Pomerance & Breines, Architects; Albin Associates, Planners)

The most common means for getting from one level to another is the stair. The plazas and public places of older cities, throughout the world, contain stairways which are admired for their functional as well as graceful design. Architects and sculptors gave much attention to stairways in the days when walking served as the chief means of movement. As walking opportunities declined, so did the dignity and delight of well-designed stairways.

Pedestrian districts offer new opportunities for stairway design. Stair treads and risers should be comfortable and safe. Handrails should have grips of human scale and be warm to the touch. Wood is good, but metal handrails need some form of congenial covering. The design of stair lights and landings is also important. But, of course, people will avoid even the best-designed stair unless it serves an obviously useful purpose.

Ramps, as articulation between levels, are sometimes encountered in public places. Despite their simplicity of form and function, ramps have a frequently overlooked inherent defect which may be better understood by this story.

In 1937 Simon Breines, co-author of this book, and Frank Lloyd Wright attended an architectural congress in Moscow. As the only Americans there, the two of them, though generations apart in age and outlook, were thrown closely together for several weeks. After the congress, Breines visited the International Exposition in Paris.

Some years later Mr. Wright came to New York on the occasion of the public announcement of plans for the Guggenheim Museum. The famous architect invited his young friend to lunch and the following conversation ensued:

WRIGHT: Well, Breines, New York City will

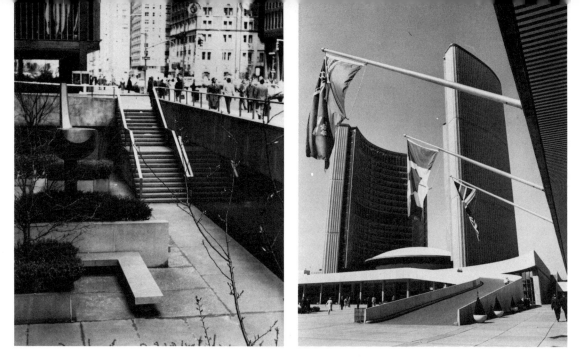

Sunken plaza (left) at the General Motors Building on Fifth Avenue, opposite the Plaza Hotel in New York City. This delightful eating area attracts restaurant customers but few other people, since the stairway leads only to a few shops and the General Motors Building basement. Midday at the McGraw-Hill sunken plaza on Sixth Avenue in New York City (middle). Not a person in sight. Pedestrians resist stairs unless the change in levels suits their convenience. Toronto City Hall (right). Since the ramp is largely aesthetic and ceremonial, people have little incentive to use it.

BREINES: finally have one of my designs. What do you think of it?

BREINES: It's exciting and impressive, of course, but the central feature of your concept troubles me.

WRIGHT: Hmm?

BREINES: When I was at the Paris Expo, I visited Le Corbusier's Pavillon d'Urbanisme. In this structure, visitors ascend a large ramp, circulate among a series of free-form platforms and leave by way of another ramp descending to the ground. Exhibits were displayed everywhere, both on the ramps and platforms.

WRIGHT: Yes, yes, what's your point?

BREINES: I noticed that people tended not to pay attention to the exhibits on the ramps going up or down. Apparently the inclines made them uneasy and anxious to get to the level as quickly as possible.

WRIGHT: Why should this interest me?

BREINES: I know you disdain any affinity with Le Corbusier, but the newspaper story shows the Guggenheim as a continuous ramp. It occurred to me that, as happened at the Pavillon d'Urbanisme, visitors would be inclined to hurry by the paintings.

WRIGHT: Do you mean to sit there and suggest that people are going to come to my museum to look at pictures?

Since both the Guggenheim Museum and the Pavillon d'Urbanisme proved to be immensely popular, the moral would seem to be to avoid ramps, unless designed by the likes of Frank Lloyd Wright or Le Corbusier.

At each depot, the loads would be broken down by building. The goods for specific buildings would be placed on modular-sized pallets which, in turn, are loaded on tractor-train cars. The nonpolluting, noiseless tractor-train then conveys the goods from the depot to each building. On arrival, the tractor-train cars with goods for a particular building are uncoupled. Each tractor-train car will be motorized for easy movement. Building entrances and freight elevators will be designed to allow tractor-train cars entry into the building with access to each floor. The entrances to new buildings will conform to pedestrian-engineering standards. With existing buildings, modifying ground-floor entrances poses no problem. Most buildings already have at least one freight elevator with extra-large doors and capacity which could accommodate tractor-train cars.

Suppose a new business tenant requires a telephone installation. The telephone company now dispatches a service truck to the job. Considerable time is spent crawling through traffic, finding curb space to park, unloading the equipment and carrying it by hand into the building. These time-wasting procedures are repeated at each job.

In a pedestrian district, the telephone company will no longer dispatch a truck. Instead, it will deliver to the transfer depot a service module designed to fit a tractor-train car. The module contains the tools and equipment needed by the telephone repairman. A tractor-train then carries the module to the designated address. First thing in the morning, the repairman arrives at the building. He rolls the fully equipped module into the service elevator and takes it to the floor where he installs the phones. After completing the job, he returns to the street with the module and places it on one of the tractor-trains regularly cruising throughout the district. Both are carried to the next repair stop. At the end of the day, he returns the module to the depot. Another fully equipped module will already have been delivered to the address of his first job the next day.

At certain hours each day, when pedestrians will suffer the least inconvenience, moving vans and other vehicles carrying loads which do not lend themselves to delivery by tractor-train will be permitted to enter the district. But most goods would travel by tractor-train. By using a form of transport that is compatible with people on foot, we keep the advantages of walking without sacrificing the services only vehicles can provide. Emergency vehicles, of course, can enter the district at any time.

We have chosen to begin this description of the fully developed pedestrian district by explaining how people and goods are moved about, because transportation is

A break in the monotonous straight-line of the gridiron street pattern brings welcome visual relief. The New York City Public Library (left) provides an admirable example of this. Where street frontages cease to determine the orientation of buildings, as in a fully developed pedestrian district, the dead-straight, open-ended street will become a thing of the past. Walking space in pedestrian districts will flow freely under and through buildings, as at 77 Water Street in New York City (right). (Emery Roth & Sons, Architects)

the shaper of cities.

Pedestrian districting will mean a different city physically. The tyranny of the gridiron pattern would end. The operation of motor vehicles necessitates the straight lines of the gridiron street system, but with conventional vehicles excluded, pedestrian districts do not need rectilinear streets and avenues, with their mean, narrow sidewalks.

Think of the entire pedestrian district as an open space at ground level. Buildings will not form canyons, with cornice lines as on a vehicular street. They will not "front" on anything, since street frontages and curbs will cease to determine the orientation of buildings. Instead, buildings will relate freely to one another, both in plan and height. They may be approached, not just by a front-street entrance, but from any side. Many of them will be open at ground level, with only the elevator and stair lobbies enclosed.

Buildings will vary in height, width and depth for the greatest penetration of light and air, and for the best visual effects. The reduction of air pollution in pedestrian districts will mean the return of the open window. Air conditioning remains a significant technological advance in urban

St. Andrews Plaza, near City Hall in lower Manhattan, opened in 1974. Because of the irregular streets in this older section of Manhattan, the alignment of buildings does not conform to the gridiron pattern of most of the city. This happy result is a consequence of historical accident. In fully developed pedestrian districts, buildings will be located freely and flexibly on the basis of design and aesthetic considerations, rather than on the rigid demands of vehicular street frontages.

comfort, but as with the automobile, we have unwisely become overly dependent on it.

High-rise towers and modest-sized structures can mingle in any desired pattern. The buildings of different sizes and shapes will resemble trees in a forest rather than, as at present, the rigid, uniform rows of an orchard. What an opportunity for architecture and urban planning!

In the absence of a conventional street system, the pedestrian district will offer walkers and mini-vehicles ample freedom of movement. This does not mean that foot and wheel will converge in disorder; instead, common-sense patterns of movement will emerge based on experience.

Dairy farmers do not try to predetermine the precise movement of their cows. Campus planners are learning this lesson. Unpredictable tribal impulses seem to determine the movement of students.* Wiser

---

* The late Louis Kahn's architectural design for the Phillips Exeter Academy library in Exeter, New Hampshire, eschewed a path to the main door in favor of an arcade around the building. "The students replied with their feet," Jane Holtz Kay writes in *The Nation*, "wearing down one quite purposeful, slightly off-kilter mud trail along the grass to the main door."

planners postpone the final layout of campus walkways until uninhibited circulation establishes clear patterns. Pedestrian planners would do well to do the same; to wait to see how use determines plan.

What the British planner Gordon Cullen calls "the art of environment" will reappear in pedestrian districts. This art thrived for centuries in cities that encouraged walking. The pedestrian is in direct contact with his environment, whereas the motorist has only a fleeting and casual relationship to it. The person on foot is conscious of building and paving materials, of lighting and signs and details of the smallest scale. The rider is more concerned with getting somewhere in the least time; for him, strong large-scale effects that can be easily and quickly grasped are what matter.

Ground level is the level which counts for the person on foot, and in a pedestrian district, that means almost everyone. Attention will be paid to the surface underfoot, paving design, street furniture, street signs and pedestrian-scale lighting.

And also to trees! With no street curbs, no damaging vehicles, no vehicular air pollution, trees and other plantings have the opportunity to survive. Instead of a single line of scraggly trees, generally found on those streets which have any trees at all, trees can be planted in double rows, and in groups—a boscage, as the

horticulturists call it. Boscage makes for parklike sitting areas and gives the architect an aesthetic component normally available only in suburban settings. The greening of cities becomes possible. Most important, a generous presence of trees will delight the pedestrian. It is difficult now to be visually aware of the changing seasons, since there are few non-park settings where one can enjoy the shade of trees in summer, and watch, as the year passes, the color of autumn leaves and the renewal of plant life in spring.

Certain forms of pedestrianism —widened sidewalks, park streets, downtown pedestrian islands, underground streets, urban strollways, for example —are feasible at this very moment. Cities already own the streets; closing them to conventional vehicles part- or full-time only requires officials with enough imagination and initiative to do so, and a public willing to support their efforts.

Compared to these proposals, the fully developed pedestrian district of the future, covering entire sections of cities and involving major problems of land assemblage, may seem to the reader like a quantum leap.

Fortunately, laws respond to the needs of the times. Many existing planning concepts can be expanded to advance the goals of pedestrianism. These include incentive zoning, discussed in Chapter IV in con-

Opened in 1953, this pedestrian district with numerous shops and restaurants—the Lijnbaan —is located in the center of Rotterdam. In addition to the more visible details of design such as paving, lighting and planting, the Lijnbaan is consciously planned to produce the exhilarating effect of surprise, something pedestrians rarely experience along the grid-iron street.

The three sketches by the British planner Gordon Cullen illustrate how the Lijnbaan designers worked their magic. The first drawing suggests the stroller's discovery of the entrance to this pedestrian area. The portal design encourages further exploration, but does not immediately reveal the scale and character of the enclosed space.

In the second sketch, the stroller enters the pedestrian area and finds himself in a relatively narrow shopping street. But already he senses that there is more here than meets the eye, for he is now aware of the Town Hall and the probability of a larger space in front of it.

In the third drawing, the pedestrian comes upon the largest of the open areas and is for the first time fully aware of the major shops, the office buildings and the old Town Hall, with its memorial sculpture group.

The visual experience suggested by this series of sketches is a pleasure only strollers can enjoy. The motorist is denied such intimate urban impressions. (Source: "A Study of Rotterdam" by Gordon Cullen, commissioned by Alcan Booth Industries Limited)

The photograph shows a Lijnbaan street scene, with the Town Hall in the background.

nection with thru-block walkways, land banks, condemnation and the transfer of development rights.

Land bank is the popular name for a municipal land reserve. Cities in the United States usually start off by owning considerable amounts of land, much of which is then sold to developers, and acquire additional land parcels by transfer from the state or federal governments, or by foreclosure of tax-delinquent properties. Many cities follow the policy of auctioning off land for which there seems to be no immediate specific public use, in order to restore it to the tax rolls. But others have learned the wisdom of depositing surplus public property into a land bank and keeping it there "to assure," in the words of Roger Starr, now Administrator of New York City's Housing Development Administration, "its dedication to those purposes which will best serve the city's present and future needs."[1] A land reserve can provide a ready and powerful means for achieving planned development.*

Condemnation as a technique of land

Landmark buildings, such as the Villard Houses in New York City, designed by McKim, Mead & White, were never intended to serve as automobile parking lots. In vehicle-free areas, landmarks will be restored to the original dignity, and strollers, not bedeviled by traffic, will have easier access to them.

assembly is often used by government for public improvements, such as slum clearance and urban development. In the future, it may be possible for municipalities to assemble land by the exercise of eminent domain and resell it to private developers who would be under an obligation to develop the area in accord with the local plan for pedestrianism.

The transfer of development rights is another technique for implementing advanced pedestrian districts. New legislation in New York City is aimed at preserving landmark buildings endangered by the pressure of rising land values. The landmark owner rightfully desires to obtain the fair market value of his property. Under the law, the landmark owner can now sell the unused development rights, permitted by the zoning, to the owner of a nearby site.

---

* Mountain Lakes, New Jersey, is an example of a suburban land bank. In the 1960s the town learned that several golf clubs within its boundaries were planning to sell out to developers. The town purchased the land with funds raised by a local bond issue. While town officials prepared a plan for the area, the land was temporarily leased back to the golf clubs. The town regained the purchase cost by selling portions of the land to builders, who were obliged to build in conformity with the town plan.

THE PEDESTRIAN REVOLUTION

Although the technique of transfer of development rights is designed for the preservation of landmarks in cities, and to preserve open spaces in suburban and rural areas, it can serve as a useful tool in furthering advanced pedestrian districts. It will permit a more flexible distribution of building bulk in a pedestrian area, and better circulation of air and penetration of sunlight. Any property owner whose development rights are not fully realized would be able to obtain the fair and full market value of his property by selling his unused development rights for transfer to other sites within the pedestrian district in accordance with the overall plan.

The scale of urban physical change over the past quarter century, accompanied by major innovations in urban development techniques, has been greater than any in history. The next quarter century is likely to bring equally dramatic changes. Among them will be significant new methods for realizing the fully developed pedestrian district—development tools not even foreseeable at the present time. For guiding these changes, Colin Buchanan offers this invaluable advice:

I would say to city designers and transportation experts: Start by considering the needs of walkers and all the subtleties that derive therefrom, work outwards from this and you will find that many other matters will fall into place, and you will not have missed the essential humanities of urban design.

These thoughts about fully developed pedestrian districts are not as definitive as Man Ray's futuristic effects in the Hollywood version of H. G. Wells's *War of the Worlds,* with their multilevel, high-speed aerial highways, and advanced air-cushioned, jet-propelled or vacuum-activated transportation systems. Pedestrianism may nevertheless provide a more realistic glimpse into the future. Whatever else the future may hold, one thing is certain: we know that the human scale will not become obsolete, and while we cannot plan for the unknown technology of the future, we can plan for the pedestrians of the future.

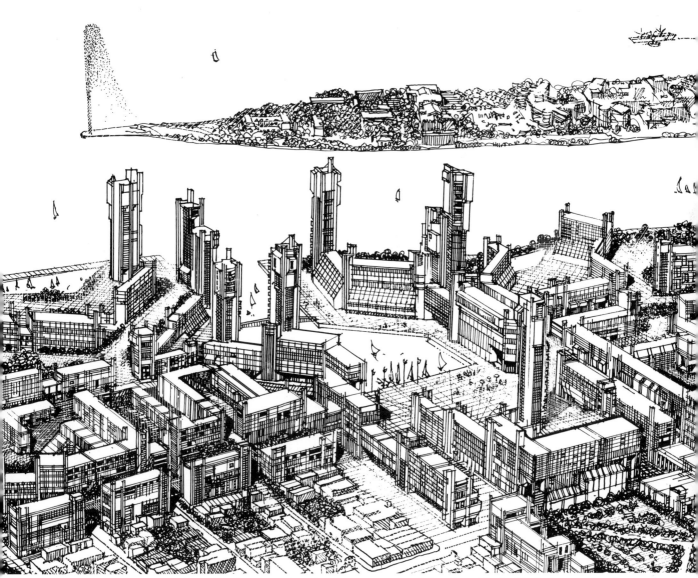

East Point, a pedestrian district, is a development proposed for New York City's borough of Queens. In the background is the southern tip of Roosevelt Island, formerly Welfare Island. Across the East River is the United Nations. East Point would cover about 300 acres and would have 60,000 residents. Residents would arrive by subway (a single stop from Grand Central Station), bus, ferry, or cars to be parked in garages at the periphery of the district. Goods and services would be brought to East Point from the landward side via a finger system of vehicular streets which dead-end short of the waterfront area. The spaces between the fingers, the marina and the waterfront park are pedestrian areas. An existing lagoon is retained to create a modern-day Piazza San Marco. (Pomerance & Breines, Architects)

CHAPTER VIII
PEDESTRIANISM IN SUBURBIA

Close to one half of the population of the United States lives in the suburbs. Since World War II, the growth of the suburbs has been phenomenal. Families who choose a suburb over the city are attracted by the greenery and open space; owning their own home; sending their children to a less troubled public school system; and finding relief from traffic congestion, pollution and crime. For some, the suburbs fulfill these expectations; others have been disappointed.

The desire to escape from the turmoil of cities to the tranquillity of the surrounding countryside is not new. The railroad, however, and later the automobile, did enable a far wider economic range of families to do what in an earlier period only the aristocracy and merchants could undertake.

The Butler Woods section of the Bronx River Parkway, within the village of Scarsdale, twenty miles from New York City. Commuters can use the path to reach the Hartsdale and Scarsdale railroad stations.

In some places, suburban walking is respected and encouraged. Note the attractive protective barriers.

Along each new railroad line, residential communities underwent rapid expansion. Most houses were built within walking distance of stations, with the more affluent venturing still farther out by horse and carriage. On maps, the early suburbs resemble a human hand, with development along the fingers, and ample open areas, much of it farmland, in the spaces between.

The automobile, flexible and fast, able to overcome all geographical constraints, altered this pattern. Instead of the relatively dense development near rail stations, in the form of garden apartments and small house lots of ten and more to the acre, the new suburbs consisted in-creasingly of individual, one-story houses on large lots of five or fewer to the acre. The open areas extending beyond the station towns filled rapidly. Zoning regulations aimed at preserving the natural environment and restricting residency to those who could afford large lots reinforced this low-density pattern.

Suburban sprawl places a heavy burden of daily travel on its residents. The suburban husband often has a long and tiring journey to get to work, usually by car. (Eight out of ten people travel to work by car in the United States.) The suburban wife spends much of her day in an automobile, chauffeuring children, shopping and running errands.

A not untypical Lexington, Massachusetts, family has this travel schedule:

For the husband, a 16-mile car trip to his Boston office.

For the wife, a 4-mile trip from home to the supermarket; 4.5 miles to the school their daughter attends; 5.1 miles to the community college where the wife takes courses; and 5.1 miles to a shopping center for non-food purchases.[1]

This pattern repeats itself in suburban communities across the country.

Vertical concentration in urban centers cripples the effectiveness of the automobile; horizontal spread in the suburbs makes it essential. "If the auto were to disappear tomorrow," states a Regional Plan Association study, "a large part of the U.S. population would be literally unable to survive, to get to work, even to buy food."[2] Thus even the awesome combination of energy shortages, higher fuel costs and heightened environmental concern is not likely to have any immediate impact on transportation in the suburbs. No alternatives to the automobile now exist. Pedestrianism can help change this, for it has an important transportation role in the suburbs, as in the cities.

Many suburbs discourage walking by the most effective means known: lack of sidewalks. Sidewalks are believed to tarnish the rural character of suburbia; indeed, walking is considered a suspicious activity. "The proprieties of an automobile civilization make walking in the suburbs a social crime," writes Simeon Strunsky.[3] Young people out on a stroll are sometimes stopped by the police, who regard their behavior with apprehension. (The Los Angeles police also have a record of halting walkers, among them the late Aldous Huxley and the science-fiction writer Ray Bradbury, with the demand that they identify themselves as responsible citizens or spend the night in jail as vagrants.[4]) Suburbanites may use their legs

Blinking lights and legible signs give suburban pedestrians a break when crossing this fast-traveled road.

for tennis or gardening, but not for walking!

This has not always been so. When the

Where a roadbed has to be lowered to avoid a steep grade, it is not necessary to alter the level of the sidewalk. Here, with salutary results, the road designer has allowed the footpath and trees to remain at the original ground level.

Bronx River Parkway, which runs thirty miles north from the New York City line to Kensico Dam in Westchester County, was built in 1925 as the first scenic auto road in the nation, pedestrians were not ignored. A fine footpath, separated physically and visually from the roadway, and with numerous footbridges over a winding stream, connected several suburban towns. Over the years, however, as traffic pressures grew, the roadbed of the Bronx River Parkway was widened and straightened to permit faster speeds. The footpath has been all but obliterated in the process, and the wooden bridges allowed to decay. In response to the protests of local civic groups, a former parkway commissioner retorted, "We can't afford to spend money on paths for a handful of pedestrians!" The commissioner conveniently forgot that the footpaths were popular with pedestrians until sacrificed for the convenience of motorists.*

If convenient and pleasant sidewalks and footpaths were provided, many of the suburbanites who live within a ten-to-fifteen-minute walk of a rail station or a bus stop, or the local shops, could walk. Side-

---

* Bridges have suffered a similar decline in pedestrian facilities. New York City's older bridges—the Brooklyn, Manhattan, Williamsburg, Queensboro and George Washington—all have footways, but bridges built in more recent years—the Tappan Zee and Verrazano—have none. On these bridges, it is not only unsafe but illegal to walk.

Respect for trees is shown by designing the sidewalk around them, and placing them well back from the curb.

walks which parallel the roadbed are better than none, and can be improved by planted separation strips, which should include trees. The sidewalks can vary in width and elevation from the roadway, as topography suggests. Ideally, suburban footways will diverge from the roadway whenever possible, and follow their own natural route. Sidewalks and footpaths can circumvent trees, large rocks and mounds. The attractive routes for footways, along drainage streams, are frequently the shortest.

Bicycles are another alternative to automobile use in the suburbs. Earlier, we described the upsurge of interest in city bike use, and the frustration of this genuine people's movement because of the dangers of street traffic. One would think that in the suburbs, bicycles could be operated in a safe and convenient manner. Not at all!

Scarsdale is a suburb of New York City, with a centrally located high school no more than a mile and a half from most parts of the village. The bicycle should be the ideal means of transportation for large numbers of its students. Yet a recent study of student travel habits by the school's Social Sciences Department reveals that 40 percent of the students use autos to travel to school, and a mere 20 percent use bikes. (The balance of students live close enough to walk, or arrive by bus.) The astonishing fact that twice as many students drive to school as bicycle is explained by the study conclusion that "students rated bikes the lowest in safety" of all possible forms of transportation. Those who chose to ride bikes to school were willing, in the words of the report, to "risk the consequences." The risk stems from the danger of fast-moving vehicles, and traveling along poorly lit streets in the early morning and at dusk; the consequences include injury and death. (In cities, at least, the lighting is better, and high vehicle densities reduce speed levels.)

The creation of safe suburban bikeways is essential. Safe bikeways are paths physically separate from road traffic. Bicycle lanes painted on traffic roads do not afford enough protection in this high-speed age. The suburban bicyclist, like his city counterpart, should not have to compete with autos and trucks for a right of way. The bikeway would link up with railroad stations, bus stops, local shops and schools. Convenient bike parking facilities should be made available at each of these sites.

Scarsdale railroad station. A one-acre parking space would be needed to accommodate the same number of cars.

Bike paths separate from footways are the ideal solution, but a shared system of paths is safer than continued road use. Tricycle riders should also be permitted on the bikeway. The criterion for use is a maximum speed of fifteen miles per hour.

A complete foot- and bicycle-path system in an existing suburban area will take time to achieve, but if an over-all plan is agreed upon, sections can be built in stages. Most local governments in suburban areas already own rights of way along the streets, and necessary property or easements can be acquired from time to time by purchase or by power of eminent domain. Potential bikeway users, both adults and children, should be involved in

the bikeway planning process, and educational efforts undertaken to stress the conservation, health and economic advantages of this means of transportation.

Traffic engineers know that new roads and highways not only take care of present needs but also generate additional traffic. The number of cars is directly related to the ability to use them. By the same token, the provision of footpaths and bikeways will encourage walking and cycling. We already know the reverse is true: where facilities are denied, as they have been, little of either is done.

But walking or cycling may not suit everyone. The aged and infirm, along with young children, also need an alternative to the automobile, as do people whose predi-

lections stop short of exercise. For such people, the mini-bus and passenger tractor-train can perform a useful role. Experimenting with these versatile vehicles is easy. The mini-bus carries ten to fifteen passengers. Its small size makes it far better suited for suburban use than the conventional bus, which is more appropriate for intercity travel and use in urban centers. Mini-buses and tractor-trains could circulate periodically through residential streets, connecting with railroad stations, express-bus stops and shops. Different routes should be tested. Fares might be subsidized partially or completely to help wean suburbanites from their cars.

Suburbanites are already accustomed to receiving deliveries, purchased from numerous stores, by a single United Parcel Service truck. Instead of the mass of trucks used by the post office, hardware, drug and grocery stores, deliveries could be made by goods-carrying tractor-trains cruising through the neighborhood. In short, sub-

Cluster development has advantages over the traditional suburban subdivision, with each house on a separate lot. In this example, clustering makes available five times more open space and involves less expenditure of funds for streets and sewer lines. (Source: New York State Department of Environmental Conservation)

CONVENTIONAL SUBDIVISION

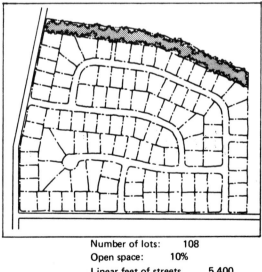

Number of lots:	108
Open space:	10%
Linear feet of streets	5,400
Linear feet of sewer lines	5,400

OPEN SPACE SUBDIVISION

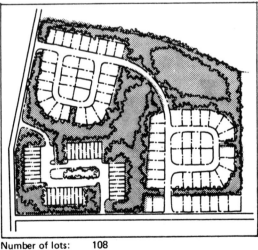

Number of lots:	108
Open space:	50%
Linear feet of streets	4,900
Linear feet of sewer lines	3,900

Map of St. George, Vermont (top), showing clustered housing and open spaces in the town center. (Robert Burley Associates, Architects)

View of St. George town center (right). (Robert Burley Associates, Architects)

New planning techniques, such as the transfer of development rights, are being tried out in exurban and rural areas in an effort to avoid suburban sprawl, with its overdependence on the automobile. For example, in Vermont the tiny town of St. George is feeling the pressure of expansion from nearby Brattleboro. A local resident of St. George, Armand J. Beliveau, has conceived of a way to develop a town center without doing harm to the still-unspoiled surrounding countryside. The idea is to require potential developers who wish to build on town-owned land to purchase development rights from surrounding landowners, mainly farmers. These landowners would thus be compensated for keeping their property in its present rural condition, and the new building development in the town center would be concentrated according to plan. By this ingenious method, the open countryside is preserved, walking is enhanced in the town center, and some mass transportation becomes possible.

urban mini-vehicle use can cut down on the number of individual trips through a rationalized transportation and delivery system and thus help reduce suburbia's prodigious expenditure of energy.

Except in the older sections near railroad stations, single-house development has made suburbia overly dependent on the automobile. The future development in existing suburbs of attached houses and garden apartments would do much to reduce this dependence, conserve energy, enhance the environment and put an end to what Mumford calls the absurd belief that space and rapid locomotion are the chief ingredients of a good life. This can be achieved by clustering dwelling units, which would not necessarily mean a higher population density in a given area.

As an example, a site of fifty acres zoned for half-acre lots would normally have a hundred individual homes built uniformly over the entire area. Under clustering, there would still be a hundred homes, but the buildings might cover only a quarter of the site. This concentration of buildings leaves more of the ground open and unspoiled. It is also more economical of sewers, water pipes and other utilities, and reduces the amount of road space needed. The cluster principle makes possible the greater use of the cul-de-sac—a dead-end street off the main road. This planning device keeps the space behind the buildings free of vehicular traffic and provides opportunity for foot paths and bikeways free of street crossings.

Those who have the means may prefer

to live in individual houses on large lots, but zoning restrictions that dictate this pattern of development will have to be eased under the pressure of population growth and the continuing exodus from

Tapiola is one of Finland's best-known new towns. In its business and residential areas, pedestrians and vehicles use separate routes.

the central city. At the present time the suburbanite has no choice. The zoning makes almost everyone live in free-standing houses; this requires each family to have one or more cars. The future suburb will give more choice of dwelling types as well as transport.

The principles of pedestrianism—separation of wheel and foot, reducing dependence on the automobile through alternative modes of transport, and reducing travel by bringing work and residence closer—can be fully achieved in new towns which are planned with these objectives from the start. Partially realized American examples are Radburn, New Jersey, designed in the 1920s by Clarence Stein and Henry Wright, and more recently, Reston, Virginia; Columbia, Maryland, and the several Rossmore Leisure Villages for retired people in California and elsewhere. Each of these towns applies a measure of restraint to the automobile. But it is the English new towns of Stevenage and Thamesmead where one finds pedestrian engineering at its most advanced.

Lying in the beautiful rolling countryside of north Hertfordshire, thirty-one miles north of London, Stevenage covers an area of 6,256 acres. Designated a new town in 1946, it now has a population of over 70,000. The separation of motor traffic, cyclist and pedestrian, is a feature of

STREETS WITHOUT CARS

Stevenage. The cycleway system incorporates underpasses at main road junctions. The all-pedestrian town center is surrounded by traffic roads forming roughly a rectangle from which access roads lead to the rear yards and loading bays of the shops and to public car parks. Housing estates are based on the Radburn, New Jersey, principle of complete separation of foot and wheel.

Thamesmead lies about eight miles east of central London on the south bank of the Thames River. To be completed in 1988, it covers 1,710 acres. The planned population is 48,000; 7,800 people are now in residence. Thamesmead will have relatively high housing densities, varying from 50 persons per acre to 140, with an average of 100 persons per acre. Planned as a complete town, not just a suburban dormitory, with industrial, commercial, residential and recreational facilities, the town design

Pedestrian plaza in Stevenage, England. The change in levels is acceptable to pedestrians because it both follows the natural grade and leads to public and play areas.

Pedestrian walks and cycle paths in Thamesmead, located eight miles east of London on the Thames River.

emphasizes footpower as a means of movement.

Thamesmead will feature a footpath network for pedestrians and possibly also for cyclists. The pedestrian routes are being as carefully designed as the routes for vehicles. They will run independently of the roads, through open land, and over and under roads. Footpaths will serve schools, shops and playing fields so that movement on foot throughout the whole town will be pleasant and safe.

Separation of foot and wheel in the town's center is achieved by a system of raised pedestrian walks related to shops and building entrances at a level above vehicular traffic. No cars need be left in the street, since there will be parking areas, open or covered, for every vehicle.

Walking conditions in Thamesmead are deliberately varied from direct routes between points to meandering paths for pleasure. Underfoot the surface alternates from paving to brick, so the quality of the street is subtly altered as one walks. Attention is given to lighting, street furniture, and insulation from noise and weather by means of planting and topography. Resting places and viewpoints occur frequently in the many areas which remain in their natural state, for the clustered housing leaves much land open.

Stevenage and Thamesmead represent important advances in the humanistic design of new towns. Yet far more suburbanites live in areas now based completely on automobile scale and use. These existing suburban areas represent an even greater challenge and opportunity for pedestrian engineering.

CHAPTER IX
THE PEDESTRIAN ADVOCATE

War is too important to be left to generals. The same can be said of transportation and traffic engineers. Departments of traffic, along with those of police, sanitation and public works, are supposed to be concerned with the well-being of the person on the street. Within the area of their special competence, this may be so, but the pedestrian is not of prime importance to any of them. We need to ensure that foot-power becomes a major concern of local government. This can be achieved by the creation of a local Department of Pedestrians, with a *Pedestrian Advocate* at its head.

Experimentation is unique to pedestrian engineering. Here the Bronx River Parkway in Westchester County, New York, becomes a bikeway for the day. Everyone seems to be observing the speed limit, probably for the first time in the parkway's history. Westchester, planning for an extensive bikeway system, closely monitors experiments like these.

The duties of the Pedestrian Advocate would be to identify areas suitable for pedestrianism; develop and implement proposals for pedestrian islands and pedestrian districts, working in close consultation with community leaders; and monitor and evaluate pedestrian experiments.

Balzac writes that streets have a physiognomy of their own. In establishing priority areas for pedestrianism, the Pedestrian Advocate should examine factors such as the nature and volume of a street's pedestrian and vehicular traffic; the environmental impact of the latter on the former; the character of the area; and the availability of transportation alternatives to the automobile. Streets with heavy pedestrian concentrations, accessible by alternate means of transportation, are prime candidates for pedestrianism.

Essential to the success of pedestrian engineering, and a requisite of a democracy, is close and continuing consultation with the people who may be affected by the experiment. Consultation can take numerous forms: meetings, questionnaires, street interviews. Local representatives of pedestrians, automobile drivers, shopkeepers and residents, along with planners and police officials, should be among those brought into the discussions. Consultations should begin early in the planning stage, to help shape the experiment, and should

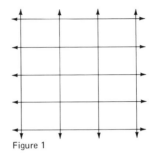

Figure 1

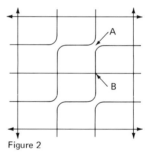

Figure 2

Detail A

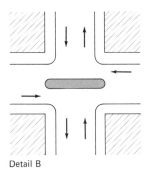

Detail B

Efforts are under way in San Francisco to reduce the harmful effect of traffic in city neighborhoods, by the designation of what are termed Protected Residential Areas. In such areas, through traffic is to be carried on collector streets designed for this purpose, and will be discouraged on residential streets by making them noncontinuous. Once traffic is reduced, there will be opportunities to modify residential streets by providing landscaping and sitting space. This technique can be a first step toward the creation of residential traffic-free pedestrian areas.

Figure 1 shows the typical gridiron street pattern found in San Francisco and most other cities, where each street carries local and through traffic.

Figure 2 shows a modification of existing streets to discourage through traffic. This can be achieved at minimum cost by means of temporary traffic barriers, and later, by the use of landscaped strips, as at "A" and "B."

Detail "A" shows the full diversion of traffic by use of landscaped strips.

Detail "B" shows a partial diversion.

continue through the experimental period and its evaluation.

The experimental process is unique to pedestrian engineering. Any street can be closed temporarily with ease and economy by the use of wooden police barriers.* If the results are favorable, the project can proceed to a more permanent form. If they

---

* A wooden barrier can achieve impressive results, as the following story in the *New York Times* indicates. On East 72nd Street in New York City a steel plate in the roadbed became dislodged, causing a fearful nighttime clatter each time an automobile passed over it. Five policemen could not push the plate back into place. *Times*

In 1958, Washington Square Park had a roadway running through its center.

are negative, the project can be modified or dropped, and little is lost.

Gadgetry such as "people movers," involving enormous outlays of funds, do not lend themselves to experimentation. If they prove wrong, and many do, their costly failure endures. A case in point is the Boeing Company "people mover" in

man John Corry went on to describe the scene that followed: "A woman in a long pink dress emerged from an apartment house. She was walking purposely, and she was carrying an old kerosene lantern. She went to a wooden sawhorse that a builder had left on the street, picked it up, and marched to the pothole. Silently, she hung the old kerosene lantern on the wooden sawhorse, and placed it over the pothole. The next car to come along swerved around the sawhorse, of course, and so did all the other cars after that. Then the woman in the pink dress went back to her apartment, and the policemen, recognizing a good thing when they saw it, left, too."

Morgantown, West Virginia, designed to transport students of West Virginia University between three separate campuses. To date, the project cost is $57 million. The original cost estimate of $13.4 million has risen to a projected final price in excess of $115 million. Actually, it is misleading to cite this as a failure which will endure, since present plans are to dynamite the 2.2 miles of elevated concrete guideway now in place.[1] (Seven years prior to this debacle, Colin Buchanan wrote: "Personally I would not let a single aerospace engineer loose on the problems of cities until he had been given a six-months' course about cities so that he had some idea of what he was dealing with. The risk, otherwise, is that money and effort will be expended on producing movement systems which, when put to the test, satisfy no known human desires for movement.")

Washington Square Park, a seven-acre park at the southern terminus of Fifth Avenue in New York City, is an excellent example of the experimental process in operation. In the mid-1950s, city officials proposed replacing an existing roadway through the park with a major depressed highway. Residents of the area, opposed to both the proposed highway and the existing roadway, recommended closing the park to vehicles altogether. Though forewarned by the New York City Planning Commission's dire prophecy that the

Washington Square Park today: vehicle-free and people-full.

blocked traffic would inundate the neighboring residential streets, the residents insisted on an experimental closing of the park roadway. Wooden police barriers were set in place. The result? No disaster whatsoever. Traffic, instead of saturating the area, sensibly took alternate routes. Later the temporary closing of the park became permanent.[2]

Experiments, however, can fail as well as succeed. Proposals to reduce dependence on motor vehicles by increasing walking possibilities will have to justify themselves by a process of demonstration, with modifications, if called for, on the basis of what is learned. The Pedestrian Advocate should monitor each experiment through interviews with pedestrians and

shopkeepers, and by surveys of pedestrian activity in the experimental area and motor-vehicle activity along nearby streets. Films of the area, before and during the experiment, and analyses of air and noise quality and the impact on sales in business districts, will provide information useful in evaluating the experiment.

Cities are unpredictable. They stubbornly resist theories and plans; thus, some pedestrian experiments will fail. Revolutionary beginnings historically are paved with failures; the Pedestrian Revolution is no exception. Failure, however, can be instructive; it all depends on what is learned, and what one does with the new-found knowledge.

Pedestrians must be considered in the context of a total strategy for movement. Mumford writes:

To have a complete urban structure capable of functioning fully, it is necessary to find appropriate channels for every form of transportation: it is the deliberate articulation of the pedestrian, the mass transit system, the street, the avenue, the expressway, and the airfield that alone can care for the needs of a modern community. Nothing less will do.[3]

To achieve this articulation, the Pedestrian Advocate will need to work closely with

Here we clearly see how a street which once cut all the way through has been interrupted to form this pedestrian plaza in Montreal.

other local government agencies: with planners, on an over-all urban movement plan for both the locality and the region; with traffic officials to work out traffic diversion routes; with mass-transportation planners, to relate the pedestrian to other modes of travel; and with police and environment officials, to ensure that pedestrians are not exposed to dangerous and unsafe conditions resulting from vehicle use.

The Pedestrian Advocate, in cooperation with employer and employee groups, could develop plans to stagger work hours, thereby reducing rush-hour congestion on city sidewalks and transportation facilities.

The Pedestrian Advocate can provide technical assistance and encouragement to residents wishing to develop a pedestrian area—for example, a block association that would like to create a park street. The Pedestrian Advocate should be aware of similar experiments in other cities, to avoid pitfalls and profit from the successes of others, as well as to fulfill the important educational function of keeping the public apprized of developments.

An important aspect of the Pedestrian Advocate's job will be reducing unnecessary movement. Communications technology, for example, is an area ripe for exploration by the Pedestrian Advocate. Closed-circuit television, cable television, picturephones and the transmission of

Street space recaptured for use by people. The closing of intersecting streets, one of which can be seen in the upper left portion of this aerial view, left) formed Glenmore Plaza in Brooklyn, New York. Emergency vehicles continue to have access to the plaza. The paving design is based on the famous sunburst of Siena's Piazza del Campo. (Pomerance & Breines, Architects; Robert Zion-Harold Breen, Landscape Architects) Ground view of Glenmore Plaza (right), showing the ample space for recreation. The fountain cools the tenants of Glenmore Plaza Houses in the summer, and in winter there can be ice skating. In all seasons, the steps around the plaza serve as a gathering place. There is constant human activity and security. (Pomerance & Breines, Architects; Robert Zion-Harold Breen, Landscape Architects)

documents—both words and pictures—by telephone hookup, can help reduce travel. The hardware for all this now exists.

The Pedestrian Advocate should encourage the rationalization of freight deliveries by expansion of the United Parcel Service concept and through the development of underground freight tunnels. The result would be thousands of fewer trucks each day congesting and polluting city streets. Why should subway systems only transport passengers? New subway lines could provide for both passenger and freight tunnels. Freight would be moved below street level by means of continuous conveyor belts, on which the goods are stationary but the belts move, or by roller track, on which the goods glide but the revolving wheels remain in place. Either system would have sub-surface access to buildings. Elevators could then carry the pallets of freight directly to the floors of a building.

The pneumatic tube works well as a delivery system in department stores, hospitals and factories. By means of a pneumatic-tube system, mail and small packages could be sent winging their way underground, further freeing streets of unnecessary vehicles. The pneumatic system could be placed in underground utility tunnels, along with water and steam mains, electric conduits, sewers, gas lines and telephone cables. The utility tunnels would be accessible to workmen from manhole or basement connections, eliminating the need for street excavations and the traffic tie-ups they cause each time a repair is required.

Providing opportunities for people to live within walking distance of their place of work is a goal of the Pedestrian Revolution. To achieve this end, the Pedestrian Advocate should be prepared to take advantage of changing urban trends. The collapse of the office-building boom in New York City is an example of how rapidly and unexpectedly urban circumstances change. The period 1960–1970 was a decade of seemingly limitless demand for commercial office space in midtown Manhattan. Neighborhoods of well-located housing were demolished to make way for new office towers. Now there is no longer a demand for more office space; indeed, the market for such space is glutted. It is timely, therefore, to consider developing sections of midtown with housing, for which there is an increasing need. A Pedestrian Advocate would use planning techniques such as incentive zoning to encourage residential mid-block walkways like 5½ Way, initially proposed in 1964 as an office-building walkway.* This

* The Fifth Avenue Special Zoning District running from 38th to 58th streets is a move in the right direction. It

downtown freight tunnel   uptown freight tunnel

A freight tunnel is one way a Pedestrian Advocate can eliminate a substantial number of trucks from city streets. This drawing shows a freight tunnel, proposed in 1950, to be built as part of New York City's Second Avenue subway. The plan was to distribute freight from uptown and downtown terminals by means of continuous conveyor belts or roller tracks, with direct, sub-surface access to buildings on or near Second Avenue. Elevators designed for the purpose would carry pallets of freight to the building floors. (Planning study by Pomerance & Breines, Architects)

would achieve four worthy objectives: more housing; reducing, for many, the length of their journey to work; the creation of a traffic-free pedestrian avenue; and twenty-four-hour activity in an area which is dead after 6 P.M.

An increasing number of Americans are disturbed by the imbalance in our consumption of energy resources. With only 6 percent of the world's population, the United States uses 35 percent of the world's energy capacity. Reducing energy use requires fundamental changes in our style of living. Criticism and exhortation alone will not alter this situation. Telling the suburbanite to drive less won't help if the automobile is the only practical means to reach work or to shop. Telling an urban resident to forgo using his car in the city is of doubtful value if alternatives like decent mass transportation and safe walkways and bikeways are not available. The mandate of Pedestrian Advocates—to increase pedestrian opportunities in urban centers and suburbia, to reduce urban

seeks to encourage developers to provide both living accommodations in the area and retail space along the avenue in place of bank and airline offices. (The latter tend to detract from the avenue's retail atmosphere.) Buildings put up in the special district must rent the lower two floors to retail merchants. If developers provide more than two floors, they become eligible for a zoning bonus. These extra floors must be used for apartments or hotel rooms. There is an additional space bonus for a developer incorporating a pedestrian arcade in the building design.

travel by encouraging work-residence districts, to encourage alternative means of travel to the automobile—points the way to these necessary changes in life style.

Pedestrianism will not arrive without controversy. Objections will always be raised to the closing of a street, no matter how congested, inconvenient or unhealthy vehicular traffic may be. Property owners have an instinctive fear of change. Shopkeepers foresee a drop in sales, and some business leaders regard traffic congestion as an indication of economic vitality—"It's good for us!" These fears, justified or not, are real, and cannot be ignored. Close consultation with these groups by the Pedestrian Advocate, and the experimental process, which permits testing pedestrian proposals before any final decisions are made, can do much to overcome these fears. But to transform the goals of the Pedestrian Revolution into reality, the Pedestrian Advocate will also need strong support from the constituency he represents—pedestrians.

Auto companies and drivers recognized early in the industry's infancy the value of organization. A few small auto companies by themselves could not hope to fend off persecution by the manufacturers of carriages or entrenched investors in trolley-car lines, but an auto club could. When auto clubs asked the government to pave roads, the politician who failed to heed

them did so at his peril. Today, when a roadbed is considered too narrow, auto interests do something about it. And one of the things they do is pare a few more feet off the sidewalks. (In one four-year period cited by Jane Jacobs, 453 roadbeds were widened in Manhattan alone by nibbling at their sidewalks.)

Until recently, pedestrians have meekly made do with the scraps left to them. Lacking organized strength, though large in number, pedestrians exert almost no influence. Bicycle riders share the same plight. Thus it comes as no surprise that in power-conscious New York City, bicyclists receive booklets on traffic safety but no affirmative action in the form of bikeways separate from motor vehicles, and

Foot walks, not the usual highway, line both sides of this river in San Antonio, Texas. Restaurants and cafés thrive in a pedestrian setting.

The Brooklyn Heights Promenade, New York (top). Waterfronts provide ideal opportunities for pedestrianism. The Phipps Garden Apartments in Queens County in New York City (right) were designed in 1931 by Clarence Stein. Now, forty-three years later, young planners are rediscovering this innovative project. "Why can't contemporary apartments be as pleasant as Phipps?" they ask. "Why does today's housing so often take the form of tall towers set in parking lots?" The answer is that when Phipps was designed, the automobile did not yet dominate the planning process. This enabled Stein to use all the available space on the site for attractive gardens. Today the automobile exerts an overwhelming, largely negative, impact on city planning.

pedestrians are left to fend for themselves.

Pedestrians and bike riders are foot-power allies. Like any other group seeking change in our society, they need to orga-nize and develop public and political sup-port. The Bill of Rights for Pedestrians can provide a rallying point. It is the manifesto of the Pedestrian Revolution.

THE PEDESTRIAN BILL OF RIGHTS

- The city shall not harm the pedestrian.
- The streets belong to all the people, and shall not be usurped for the passage and storage of motor vehicles.
- People shall have the right to cycle in safety; that means ample provision of bikeways separate from trucks, buses and automobiles.
- To reduce dependence on the automobile, city and suburban residents shall have the right to convenient, clean and safe mass transportation.
- People shall be freed from the heavy burdens of daily travel by having the opportunity to live near their places of work.
- Urban residents shall have plentiful and generous open public places—outside of parks—for gathering and ceremonies.
- Pedestrians shall have the right to breathe clean air on streets, free of the harmful fumes of vehicles.
- Standing room only on city streets shall end by providing benches for sitting and relaxation.
- The sounds of human voices shall replace vehicular noise on city streets.
- Concern for the welfare of pedestrians shall extend to the surface under foot—with paving congenial for walking—and shall include human-scale street furniture and signs.
- Urban man shall have the right to experience trees, plants and flowers along city streets.
- Cities shall exist for the care and culture of human beings, pedestrians all!

NOTES

1 The Pedestrian Revolution

1. Bernard Rudofsky, *Streets for People* (New York: Doubleday, 1969), p. 115.

2. Lewis Mumford, *The City in History* (New York: Harcourt, Brace & World, 1961; A Harbinger Book, 1961), p. 550.

3. Henry Ford, "America's Motorcracy," the *New York Times* (November 28, 1973), p. 45.

4. Don C. Miles, "Why Pedestrian Streets Succeed," in Roberto Brambilla, ed., *More Streets for People* (New York: The Italian Art and Landscape Foundation, 1973), p. 98.

5. This definition of a pedestrian was coined by Simeon Strunsky, for many years the "Topics of the Times" columnist for the *New York Times*.

6. *Walking Space in City Centers,* an interim report summary of the Regional Plan Association (New York: Regional Plan Association, 1971), p. 15.

7. *GLC Study Tour of Europe and America: Pedestrianised Streets* (London: Greater London Council, 1973), p. 40.

8. *Citizen's Policy Guide to Environmental Priorities for New York City 1974-1984,* an interim report (New York: Council on the Environment of New York City, 1973), p. 17.

9. Lawrence Galton, *Outdoorsman's Fitness and Medical Guide* (New York: Harper & Row, 1966), p. 9.

2 The Pedestrian in History

1. Bernard Rudofsky, *Streets for People* (New York: Doubleday, 1969), p. 83.

2. Lewis Mumford, *The City in History* (New York: Harcourt, Brace & World, 1961; A Harbinger Book, 1961), p. 194.

3. *Ibid.,* p. 541.

4. Juvenal, *Juvenal and Persius,* Loeb Classical Library, pp. 48–51.

5. Mumford, *op. cit.,* p. 212.

6. *Ibid.,* p. 302.

7. Fritz Rörig, *The Medieval Town* (Berkeley: University of California Press, 1967), pp. 172–173.

8. Will Durant, *The Age of Faith* (New York: Simon & Schuster, 1950), p. 302.

9. Joan Evans, *Life in Medieval France* (Oxford: Oxford University Press, 1925), p. 75.

10. Mumford, *op. cit.,* p. 384.

11. Henry S. Churchill, *The City Is the People* (New York: Reynal & Hitchcock, 1945), p. 20.

12. Mumford, *op. cit.,* p. 370.

13. *Ibid.,* pp. 426–427.

14. H. B. Creswell in the *Architectural Review* (December, 1958), as quoted in Jane Jacobs' book, *The Death and Life of Great American Cities* (New York: Random House, 1961; Vintage Books, 1961), p. 341.

NOTES

3 Urban Pedestrian Islands

1. *New York's City Streets: A Guide to Making Your Block More Lively and More Livable* (New York: The Council on the Environment of New York City, 1973), pp. 31-32.

2. Jane Jacobs, *The Death and Life of Great American Cities* (New York: Random House, 1961; Vintage Books, 1961), p. 72.

3. William A. Caldwell, ed., *How to Save Urban America* (New York: Regional Plan Association, 1973), pp. 131-132.

4. Emma Rothschild, *Paradise Lost: The Decline of the Auto-Industrial Age* (New York: Random House, 1973).

5. *GLC Study Tour of Europe and America: Pedestrianised Streets* (London: Greater London Council, 1973), p. 187.

6. Caldwell, *op. cit.*, p. 73.

7. Don C. Miles, "Why Pedestrian Streets Succeed," in Roberto Brambilla, ed., *More Streets for People* (New York: The Italian Art and Landscape Foundation, 1973), p. 99.

8. *GLC Study Tour . . ., op. cit.*, p. 103.

9. *Ibid.*, p. 101.

4 Urban Pedestrian Districts

1. Charles Mulford Robinson, *City Planning, With Special Reference to the Planning of Streets and Lots* (New York: Putnam's, 1916), p. 18.

2. Lewis Mumford, *The City in History* (New York: Harcourt, Brace & World, 1961; A Harbinger Book, 1961), p. 422.

3. Jane Jacobs, *The Death and Life of Great American Cities* (New York: Random House, 1961; Vintage Books, 1961), p. 185.

4. The *New York Times* (November 26, 1973).

5. Douglas Haskell, "Unity and Harmony at Rockefeller Center," *The Architectural Forum* (January/February, 1966).

6. Mumford, *op. cit.*, p. 429.

7. Gordon Cullen, *The Concise Townscape* (New York: Reinhold, 1961), p. 103.

8. Albert Mayer, *The Urgent Future* (New York: McGraw-Hill, 1967), p. 105.

9. Roger Starr, *The Living End: The City and Its Critics* (New York: Coward-McCann, 1966), p. 194.

5 The Bicycle as Urban Transport

1. Roland C. Geist, *Bicycling as a Hobby* (New York: Harper & Brothers, 1940), p. 143.

2. I. N. Phelps Stokes, comp., *The Iconography of Manhattan Island (1498-1909)*, Vol. 5 (New York: Arno Press, 1967), p. 2022.

3. *GLC Study Tour of Europe and America: Pedestrianised Streets* (London: Greater London Council, 1973), p. 113.

4. William Saroyan, *The Bicycle Rider in Beverly Hills* (New York: Scribner's, 1952), p. 12.

5. "Out of the Air: Two Wheels Good," *The Listener* (February 7, 1974), p. 179.

6. Richard Ballantine, *Richard's Bicycle Book* (New York: Ballantine Books, 1972), p. 69.

7. This figure is arrived at as follows: Manhattan's resident population totals 1.5 million. Sixty percent of this total, or 900,000 people, are in the 18-65 age group. It is assumed that 10 percent of this group—90,000 people—would be interested in the bike-rental service.

6 Other Mini-Vehicles

1. Henry Ford, "America's Motorcracy," the *New York Times* (November 28, 1973), p. 45.

7 The Fully Developed Pedestrian District

1. Roger Starr, "Vacant Land Management: A Challenge to New York City," *Fordham Law Review*, Vol. XXIX (April, 1961), p. 673.

8 Pedestrianism in Suburbia

1. The *New York Times* (July 15, 1973), pp. 1, 54.

2. William A. Caldwell, ed., *How to Save Urban America* (New York: Regional Plan Association, 1973), p. 51.

3. Simeon Strunsky, *No Mean City* (New York: Dutton, 1944), p. 163.

4. Aaron Sussman and Ruth Goode, *The Magic of Walking* (New York: Simon & Schuster, 1967), p. 37.

9 The Pedestrian Advocate

1. The *New York Times* (April 13, 1974), pp. 1, 26.

2. Jane Jacobs, *The Death and Life of Great American Cities* (New York; Random House, 1961; Vintage Books, 1961), pp. 360-362.

3. Lewis Mumford, *The City in History* (New York: Harcourt, Brace & World, 1961; A Harbinger Book, 1961), p. 508.

PHOTO CREDITS

ABOUT THE AUTHORS

SIMON BREINES is a partner of Pomerance & Breines, Architects, and a Fellow of the American Institute of Architects. His firm has designed many public and private buildings, including the proposed "5½ Way," a pedestrian mall between Fifth and Sixth avenues from 42nd Street to Central Park in New York City. Mr. Breines served as the Architect Member of the Art Commission of New York City from 1971 to 1973, and has also served as first president of the Landmarks Conservancy of New York, as President of the Scarsdale Audubon Society, and as a board member of the Municipal Art Society and the Citizens Union of the City of New York. He is co-author of *Architecture and Furniture of Alvar Aalto* (Museum of Modern Art) and *The Book of Houses* (Crown). He contributed a chapter to *Small Urban Spaces* (New York University Press), and his writings on pedestrian planning have appeared in the *Journal of the American Institute of Architects* and the *Architectural Forum.*

WILLIAM J. DEAN is a lawyer. He has served as Executive Secretary of the Citizens Union of the City of New York, a nonpartisan civic organization concerned with improvement of New York City and state government, and as an officer of the International Institute for Environmental Affairs. Mr. Dean is a member of the adult education faculty of the New School for Social Research, where he conducts an annual forum series on urban issues, and president of the Citizens Union Research Foundation.